SURVIVE!

THE DISASTER, CRISIS
AND EMERGENCY
HANDBOOK

BY
JERRY AHERN
PHOTOS BY SHARON AHERN

©2010 Jerry Ahern

Published by

kp **krause publications**

A division of F+W Media, Inc.

www.krausebooks.com

700 East State Street • Iola, WI 54990-0001
715-445-2214 • 888-457-2873

Our toll-free number to place an order or obtain
a free catalog is (800) 258-0929.

Library of Congress Control Number: 2009937524

ISBN 13: 978-1-4402-1112-6
ISBN 10: 1-4402-1112-4

Designed by Dave Hauser

Edited by Dan Shideler

Printed in the United States of America

DEDICATION

This book is respectfully dedicated to the men and women whose creativity and foresight have brought sciences such as meteorology, volcanology, seismology and others to the prediction levels thus far achieved. They save lives, often risking their own. Risk of life and limb is all in a day's work to our heroic first responders – police, fire and emergency – men and women who race to reach what others flee, all in the pursuit of helping their fellow man. And, since there are manmade disasters as well as those naturally occurring, we must never forget the men and women who daily and diligently safeguard us with their labors in the military, intelligence and law enforcement communities.

Table of Contents

Acknowledgments

"I'd like to thank the academy – " Oops! Wrong speech!

Actually, I have four "thank you's" to make concerning *Survive! The Disaster, Crisis and Emergency Handbook.* As always, this book or any book bearing the Ahern name or an Ahern pseudonym wouldn't exist except for this beautiful girl I met on my first day in high school in September of 1961. I'd talk about how intelligent Sharon is, too, except for the fact that she married me in October of 1968. Sharon has always been my best buddy, she's my co-writer on our novels and my photographer on my magazine articles and for books like this. Thanks, kid.

I'd like to thank my editor for this book, Dan Shideler. Early on, Dan got behind this idea and worked really hard to make this book a reality on the publishing schedule. He's a good guy.

I'd like to thank all the people in the outdoors and related industries who helped us with everything from data to samples we could examine and use. The creativity of these people – from conception to realization – is incredible.

Finally, I've got to mention all the good people who have read our books, our articles and our columns – over the three and one-half decades I've been getting paid to write – and keep coming back to us again and again. No words of thanks could ever be enough. You allow me to do something I love and make a living doing it. Can't beat that!

Jerry Ahern
October 7, 2009

Introduction

This is not a book about how to get ready for the "end of civilization as we know it." As a husband, a father and a grandfather, I have no interest at all in societal collapse, I do not view turmoil and chaos as exciting, and roughing it is all well and good so long as one does so by choice and, at the end of the excursion, one can return to hot showers, warm meals and soft bedding. In short, I'm not eagerly looking forward to Armageddon.

However, we must be mindful of the most important fact of life: although it is intrinsic to human nature at the most basic level to fight to survive, there are certain requirements for men and women to exist which cannot be ignored.

Under average circumstances, depending on our size and body fat, we can exist for 10 days or so without food, possibly several weeks A few days without water and the body approaches renal failure and other dehydration-related problems; make it three or four days and it means death. Few of us can go without oxygen replenishment – taking a breath – for much more than two or three minutes. Our comparatively hairless bodies require protection from excessive heat and excessive cold; we burn, we suffer heat exhaustion, we numb and pass through sleep into death. A great many of us can swim quite well and for long duration, but only a few might stay afloat for days at a time. Eight or nine days seems something like a record, and this is possible only with the aid of floating debris.

We need stuff to stay alive. By "stuff," I mean food, water, breathable air, clothing, shelter from the elements and temperature extremes, and the means by which we can protect ourselves from other living things that might do us grievous harm.

Some cataclysmic incident could well take place which would so undo the basic fabric of society that mankind might not recover for decades or even centuries, if at all. Such occurrences are life-altering, potentially life-ending, for large numbers of our fellow men. The 2004 Christmas Tsunami in Indonesia is a classic example of such a mega-tragedy, and even it was not on the global scale of a major meteor strike or a significant series of thermonuclear events. What is considerably more likely, however, is a serious disruption in the delivery system of civilization's usual amenities, one which might endure for several days, perhaps as long as several months.

It is the intent of this book to assist in enabling the reader to make it through intact to "the other side" of such temporary disruptions, to be able to get back to normal with all one's family alive and well and healthy, traumatized by whatever the events might be as little as possible.

Whether by the hand of nature, through careless accident or by evil design, disaster is inevitable. So, get ready – and survive!

Ahern with Olivia, one of his granddaughters, and Honey the Wonderdog. In the final analysis, at the heart of planning for surviving disasters, is the concept of family, the upcoming generation.

CHAPTER 1:
LIFE IN THE
21st CENTURY
A CATALOG OF IMPENDING DISASTERS

Disasters are generally classifiable as natural or manmade, this latter division further breaking down into those that are accidental and those that are intentional. A Category 4 or Category 5 hurricane making landfall is a natural disaster. The failure of a containment vessel at a thermonuclear power plant is an accidental manmade disaster. A terrorist using a "dirty bomb" is an intentional manmade disaster.

Some disasters, however grim, are quite common, really. Take the tornado. A rarity in parts of the world, a freak occurrence elsewhere, there are portions of North America where tornados occur with devastating regularity. Despite winds that may top out over 300 miles per hour, towns that may be partially or wholly destroyed, numerous horrible deaths, we get past tornados, rebuild and go on. That is the nature of most disasters. It is human nature. We pick up the pieces of our lives and start again.

A tornado as photographed by NOAA.

The Yellowstone Caldera

There are, however, true cataclysms that will someday strike, the effect of which will be staggering. Take the Yellowstone caldera, a huge "super volcano," the inevitability of the eruption of which *will* – not *might* – radically alter Earth's climate for a period of years. This eruption could start before I finish writing this sentence. The caldera measures about 30 miles wide by 50 miles long: 1500 square miles of ticking time bomb. If you live east of Yellowstone and north of the southern tier of the southeastern United States, you will evacuate southward or you will die.

The last full-scale eruption of the Yellowstone caldera was approximately

640,000 years ago. The volcano is reportedly at least 30,000 years overdue for another major eruption. The last major eruption of the caldera hurled approximately 240 cubic miles of rock and volcanic dust into Earth's atmosphere. The next eruption – which no power on Earth can prevent – will smother much of North America beneath deep drifts of volcanic ash, which turns to a concrete-like substance when it comes in contact with the moisture inside your lungs. The dust will likely shroud the entire Northern Hemisphere for years, eventually falling to Earth over a range of thousands of square miles and much of civilization will end in darkness, cold and starvation.

A caldera is a huge volcanic crater, formed by the collapse of a volcanic cone or a volcanic eruption of tremendous force. Such a caldera has come to be known by the term "supervolcano," a word coined by the BBC in conjunction with their release of a docudrama concerning Yellowstone's potential for destruction.

There are three such supervolcanos in the United States, all west of the Rockies. Yellowstone is the biggest. It last erupted 640,000 years ago. It erupts with comparative regularity, every 600,000 years. Although nothing points to imminent eruption – 1000 to 3000 earthquakes each year in Yellowstone is normal – we are quite a bit overdue for Yellowstone to go bang. When it goes bang, it will likely be the loudest noise ever heard by humankind.

During one Yellowstone eruption 2.1 million years ago, the caldera spewed *585 cubic miles of magma*, about six thousand times the magma flow from the Mt. St. Helens eruption of May 18, 1980. Think about that.

When Yellowstone goes this time, there will be a series of earthquakes, one of which will puncture the caldera and release magma. A crude comparison would be like lancing a boil, without being able to restrain the

When the Yellowstone Caldera goes up, it'll make the Mt. St. Helens eruption look like a burp. Photo courtesy FEMA News Photo.

fluid beneath. Magma would be catapulted more than 25 miles high into the atmosphere. Every human being or animal out in the open (and most indoors) would be dead within a 500- or 600-mile radius, with volcanic ash blanketing everything from Iowa to the Gulf of Mexico.

There could be as much as *500 to 600 cubic miles* of lava expelled. A like amount of volcanic ash would be propelled into the atmosphere, eventually circling the globe, knocking out the Midwestern breadbasket by covering it instantly with a layer of killing ash, within a short period of time producing the same effect over the most arable lands of the northern hemisphere. Temperatures would certainly plummet because incoming solar radiation would be blocked. There would be mass extinctions in an eerie and deadly darkness.

The scientific and pseudo-scientific communities are concerned about the Yellowstone Caldera and divided about the immediacy of an eruption. It could, indeed, happen while I'm writing this paragraph or while you are reading it; or the eruption might not take place for thousands or even tens of thousands of years. If the possibility of an eruption taking place within a few days were advanced, how could one prepare? Evacuate? There wouldn't be enough time to get even a significant minority of the persons who would be affected globally to safer climes. The only chance you, as an individual, would have to "combat" a supervolcano eruption is to keep track of what's going on at caldera sites. There are other supervolcanoes throughout the world, and Yellowstone isn't even the largest.

Earthquakes

Earthquakes are the result of plate or tectonic movement of the Earth's crust. As plates abrade against one another, there is slippage. This slippage creates upthrust, the force of which which can build mountain ranges. It also creates earthquakes.

The Great San Francisco Earthquake of 1906. Think it can't happen again?

What is likely the most deadly earthquake in human history took place in the mid-sixteenth century in China, claiming over 800,000 lives. Of all the scales by which natural disasters are measured, the Richter scale for measuring the intensity of an earthquake is the most well known, although little understood. It was developed in 1935. The difference between an earthquake measuring a 6.5 on the Richter scale and one measuring a 7.5 is not just one full "notch" higher, but rather a difference of a factor of 10 because each whole number is composed of 10 decimals. The amount of energy released is not just 10 points more or even 10 times higher, but thirty-one times greater between each whole number – the difference between a 6.5 and a 7.5, for example.

BEAR PHOTO
S.F   563

As designed by Charles F. Richter, the system has no upper limit. Earthquakes can range from those not really felt at all and measurable only by nearby seismographs to medium-range quakes which will record all over the world to the megaquakes which occur rarely. Anything below a 5.4 will cause little or no damage and may go largely or completely unnoticed. Between 5.4 and 6.0, there can be significant damage to buildings not designed to stand up to a modest quake.

An earthquake registering over 6 and under 7 is significant and damage can be widespread. Above 7 and under 8 is considered a major earthquake, signifying the potential for widespread damage. It should be remembered that the Richter scale does not measure damage, merely the strength of the quake. Where the earthquake takes place is the key component in how much damage will occur.

An 8.0 or greater temblor is a Great Earthquake and, depending on location, can take hundreds or more lives and cause a colossal amount of damage. So far, at least, the greatest earthquake ever recorded was a 9.5 and took place in Chile in 1960. Earthquakes measuring 8 and above rarely occur more than once in any given year. The earthquake that triggered the eruption of Mt. St. Helens was "only" a 5.1.

In areas where earth movement occurs regularly, building codes incorporate design requirements for withstanding a given size of earthquake. This is seen most notably in California and Japan. Areas where significant quakes have not occurred for a century or longer will not have such guidelines in their building codes. Adapting construction to withstand earthquake activity is more expensive, of course, and such will not be seen in high-rise buildings in areas where the odds are that no major quake will occur in the foreseeable future. Such is the case along the New Madrid Fault. Memphis, Tennessee, and other population centers near the fault line could suffer incalculable loss of life and property damage if a Great Earthquake struck.

Earthquake is one of the most terrifying of the ultra-serious disasters, and can, of course, be linked to other geological phenomena, such as volcanic eruptions. For generations, the "Big One" has been expected to hit Southern California. The last "big one" earthquake hit San Francisco in 1906. Several "pretty big ones" have hit California since then – like the 7.1 Loma Prieta quake – and will again. If you were to study a map showing global earthquake activity, indeed, you would find high concentrations in certain locations, southern and central California among them. All along the Pacific Rim, in fact, earthquake and volcanic activity is significant. If you view it on a map, it really does look like its name – "The Ring of Fire."

But one should not ignore the less well-known earthquake possibilities. The New Madrid Fault runs roughly north to south for an approximate distance of 150 miles, crisscrossing under the Mississippi River at least three times, starting in Southern Illinois and terminating in Arkansas. There are about 200 earthquakes of modest caliber recorded along this fault line in any given year. In 1811 and 1812, there were three earthquakes of literally earth-shaking significance, thought to have been an 8 or higher on the Richter scale, felt throughout the United States as they occurred, reportedly ringing church bells as far away as Boston. New lakes were formed while houses and fields disappeared into the ground and the course of the Mississippi River itself was altered. New Madrid will tremble above a 6 on the Richter scale again. Unlike cities like Los Angeles and Tokyo, earthquake planning does not generally figure into building construction along the New Madrid Fault.

Tsunamis

Earthquakes take place not only on dry land but under the oceans, too, perhaps miles deep within the earth. When plate tectonics (or landslides or volcanism) result in earthquakes beneath the sea, great amounts of water are displaced and coastal areas can experience tsunamis. The tsunami that took place on December 26, 2004, was the result of a 9.0 to 9.3 earthquake in the Indian Ocean with an energy level estimated to be the equivalent of *more than 20,000 atomic bombs*. It was responsible for more than 150,000 immediate deaths and disappearances (almost 230,000 lives lost in total) and it displaced millions of people in 11 countries.

Tsunamis have struck in locations as diverse as Chile, Java, Sumatra, Italy and, as recent research indicates, in the Pacific Northwest hundreds of years ago. Tsunamis can travel as rapidly as 600 miles per hour on the open sea, but are barely noticeable, perhaps only a foot or so in height, rising to monstrous proportions only as the tons and tons of displaced water approach shore.

Rocks from Space

If one of the 600 or so identified or likely even more numerous unidentified Near Earth Objects of considerable size strikes Earth – they have in the geologic past and they will again in the future – the effect on humankind could range from temporarily devastating to utterly terminal. Near Earth Objects which bombarded Earth in the past may well have carried with them the original water molecules and carbon molecules from which life may have originated. It is theory generally accepted as scientific fact that the extinction of the dinosaurs 65 million years ago, along with about 70 percent of all other species, came about as the result of a meteor thought to be approximately six miles wide that struck Earth and formed a crater which became the Gulf of Mexico, the debris hurled into the atmosphere from the impact blocking incoming solar radiation for a period of years, with temperatures falling to killingly cold lows and vegetation disappearing from large portions of the Earth's surface.

Some "space rocks" may have brought with them the building blocks of life, while others have brought death.

Large, solitary Near Earth Objects – not necessarily anywhere near as big as the one which is credited with wiping out the dinosaurs, perhaps only a few hundred feet across – or a series of smaller objects (the result of a very large object's fragmentation for whatever reason, whether naturally occurring or as a result of an unsuccessful attempt to blow up the object with a nuclear-warhead fitted missile) are capable of disproportionately enormous destruction. The really, really big ones are popularly called "Planet Killers." The name is not an exaggeration. Discussions concerning the tracking of Near Earth Objects so that humankind will have time to devise the means by which to deflect such a strike usually includes the sobering fact that, up until quite recently at least, the number of people actively engaged in locating Near Earth Objects and calculating their orbit and frequency was about the same as the full staff of a typical McDonald's. Rest easy.

The United States leads in this vital research which could mean the difference between our survival as a species and the mass extinction of mankind. That said, as this is written in 2009, NASA has recently indicated it has identified perhaps only 25 percent of significantly-sized Near Earth Objects, this despite the fact that Congress, having charged NASA with this task, has budgeted nothing for new observation equipment enabling NASA to accomplish this task. The "cash for clunkers" program was probably deemed more important.

Flu: Bird, Swine and Otherwise

Of course, there's the much discussed possibility of Global Pandemic, perhaps as the bird flu (H5N1) or the swine flu variant known as H1N1. These days, with air travel and the global nature of human society in general, even given advanced public health capabilities, the number of deaths could be vastly higher. One report credits the WHO (World Health Organization) with estimating the potential for H1N1 deaths in a full-tilt outbreak, which could be well underway as you read this, at perhaps as high as 360 million people – about as many people living in the USA.

Influenza is an increasing, yet somewhat preventable, threat throughout the entire world. Photo courtesy FEMA News Photo

As this is written, it is posited by some sources that between 30 to 50 percent of the U.S. population might contract H1N1 and that this could result in somewhere between 30,000 and 90,000 deaths. This sounds terrible and is, but put in perspective, a normal "plain old flu" season claims about 36,000 lives.

So far, H1N1 does not look like it will be a re-run of the Spanish Influenza outbreak, which took place in 1918, in the aftermath of World War I. No one seems to know the exact number, of course, but as many as 100,000,000 persons may have died as a result. That figure represents 1/16 of the Earth's population at the time.

The most lethal outbreak of all time in terms of per capita deaths, the Black Death or Great Plague of the 14th century, is estimated to have killed as many as 100 million Europeans, as much as 60 percent of that continent's population. This illness, clinically known as bubonic plague, again reared its head in London in 1665, killing 20 perecent of that city's population.

Contrary to popular belief, bubonic plague hasn't been eradicated. There have been many cases in the twentieth century, some of them in the United States.

Sobering information, isn't it?

Hurricanes

A tsunami-like tidal wave struck Bangladesh in 1991, claiming almost 140,000 lives. It was precipitated by Cyclone Marian. "Cyclone" is the term used in that part of the world for "hurricane."

Storm-chasers document incoming weather hazards but are utterly unable to prevent them. Photo courtesy NOAA

Hurricanes are measured on the Saffir-Simpson scale and are rated between a Category One through a Category Five. Wind speed is the determining factor. Hurricanes will shift up or down in wind speed due to the temperature of the water over which they travel; when traveling over dry land, hurricanes lose energy quickly – but not quickly enough. Although wind damage can be great, the principle destructive force associated with a hurricane is water, whether rising from a storm surge or falling as torrential rain.

Hurricanes and Pacific cyclones start as tropical disturbances, maturing into tropical depressions. Depressions are closed systems with wind speeds of 38 miles per hour or less. At 39 to 73 miles per hour maximum sustained surface wind speed, the phenomenon is officially a tropical storm. Tropical storms, even

Evacuees crowd the New Orleans Superdome in the wake of Hurricane Katrina.
Photo courtesy FEMA News Photo

if they never reach hurricane proportions, can bring devastating rains and 70 mile per hour winds are serious. As the storm passes the speed of 74 miles per hour, it becomes a hurricane. Hurricanes which can strike at the mainland United States along the East coast or swing up past Jamaica and Cuba, then hit the Gulf, begin off the west coast of Africa, picking up moisture and energy, traveling westward as their wind speeds increase.

A Category One hurricane has winds at 74 to 95 miles per hour and a storm surge four to five feet over normal highs. A Category Two has winds from 96 to 110 miles per hour and a surge of six to eight feet over normal. A Category Three hurricane features winds ranging between 111 and 130 miles per hour and a tidal surge nine to 12 feet above normal. A Category Four – where things

really start to get dangerous – has winds ranging between 131 and 155 miles per hour and a surge 13 to 18 feet above normal. Category Five – the greatest strength contemplated – has winds over 155 miles per hour and the surge is greater than 18 feet over normal.

Threes, Fours and Fives are major hurricanes. As this is written, only three Category Five hurricanes have made landfall in the United States since recordkeeping began. Although Hurricane Katrina was a Category Five over the Gulf of Mexico, by the time the storm made landfall, its intensity was down to Category Three.

Climate Change

People on both sides of the global warming debate, their radically different positions notwithstanding, must grant that it is natural for the Earth to go through warming periods and cooling periods. None of this is to say that the activities of mankind may or may not serve to hasten either process. But, while the debate continues, it is sensible to explore all the possibilities. Indeed, when the global warming issue first surfaced, it emerged from research that was being done on what was thought to be global cooling and worry over the threat of a new ice age.

Let's look at the facts concerning the last mini-ice age. Let's examine economic conditions for a moment, as these economic conditions are inexorably tied to societal and practical issues. Between the mid-16th and mid-19th centuries there was a cooling of Western Europe's climate that was considered rather severe. This affected the rest of the northern hemisphere directly, while indirectly impacting other locations around the world. During a mini-ice age, as this was, glaciers expand, but not greatly, and there is an overall cooling effect on the land and the water. Only during a major ice age would substantial retreat of the oceans become a factor.

Much of agriculture is routine and predicated on a degree of normalcy in the seasons and the temperatures. Once the "normalcy" is gone because temperatures are either higher or lower and the seasons are shorter and the effect of sunshine is greater or lesser, crops suffer. Try going to the store to buy orange juice in the aftermath of an unexpectedly brutal Florida winter. Prices are higher. Agriculturally, nothing is immune. The wise farmer, for example, faced with the inevitability of colder weather, will plant rye as opposed to wheat because rye will grow in conditions in which wheat will not.

Everything is interdependent and nothing stands on its own where climate is concerned. When it gets colder, people will have to move farther south in order to practice agriculture. When it grows warmer and the deserts begin to expand, people will likely move farther north. But they will move either way. If the seas fall, people are not likely to move that much closer to the ocean; but, if the seas rise dramatically, large numbers of people will be forced inland. When crops are affected by too much heat or too much cold or people are forced to give up land where they grow these crops, there is a likelihood of famine and starvation. Population relocations and a doubtful food supply lead to disease. These also lead to social unrest, as they did during the mini-ice age.

When there is a severe climate change, whether colder or warmer, all these other changes come into play. The more dramatic the changes in climate, the more dramatic are the results on the population. Is five percent of arable land affected? Or, is it 15 or 20 percent of arable land that can no longer be worked?

Consider something with which, as Americans, we should be intimately familiar. Remember reading about and seeing photos and movies of the Dust Bowl of the 1930's midwest, when rainfall was drastically reduced, crops failed and grasses could no longer hold the soil and the soil went airborne as dust? The economic tragedy was so severe that it affected an entire generation.

Whether colder or warmer, a mini-ice age or period of mini-global warming would be bad enough. There is historical data to support theories that might be developed concerning likely results for everything from agriculture to disease. But the last time there was a full blown dramatic climate change – during the last actual major ice age – such records from which meaningful data could be derived were not kept. There is the fossil record, of course, but there are no records concerning crop yields, severity of storms or anything of that nature from 14,700 years ago. If we go into a period of major change that will last for a protracted period of time, or possibly (but not likely) become permanent, we will be flying totally blind, and disaster is way too mild a word for it. The order of present-day civilization would be totally disrupted for large segments of Earth's population. Poorer nations and less urbanized populations would feel many of the effects soonest, but the cities could not exist without that which only the land can provide.

Wildfires

In 1934, the equivalent of eight city blocks was consumed in Chicago's worst fire since the Great Chicago Fire. It was called the Chicago Stockyards Fire. My mom's family lived quite a good distance south of the "Yards," but the wind was such that her dad had the hose out and kept soaking the roof of their house, lest an errant spark take hold. He wasn't an alarmist; he was just being practical.

As I am writing this, wildfires are assaulting portions of southern California near Los Angeles. The formula for a wildfire is simple. You need dry conditions – a drought is ideal – and you need combustible materials such as grass, brush or trees. Some of the dead undergrowth being consumed as this is written is reportedly 60 years old – you couldn't ask for better tinder. Then all you need is a spark.

All it takes is a spark. Photo courtesy FEMA News Photo

The spark can arise from a lightning strike, an accident, carelessness or it can be deliberately set. A campfire not properly extinguished, a cigarette butt carelessly flung from an open car window, a fire set for clearing brush that gets out of hand and spreads, someone who likes to watch things burn and thinks fires are fun – these and myriad other causes start fires that cost millions to extinguish and may destroy millions of dollars in property and can and sometimes do take human lives.

Wind, although not always necessary, helps spread the fire, driving it onward. Wind can also work with the fire to create the fire's own weather system. This is what's known as a "firestorm." The fire demands oxygen, drawing air toward itself. If it draws enough air sufficiently rapidly, it creates winds. The winds are pulled in toward the fire. Warm air rises, of course, and the wind becomes an updraft. These winds are erratic and will veer off from the heart of the system, engulfing more and more area in wind driven flame.

Either the winds associated with the main fire column itself or one of the winds veering off from the main fire or even two fires coming together may produce what is commonly called a "fire whirl." This can range in size from something that mimics a dust devil up to that of a tornado. Just like a tornado, the fire whirl can jump. Where it lands, it burns.

The firestorm feeds itself with what it consumes. As long as there are sufficient heat and sufficient fuel, the fire storm will draw in air, create winds and go on. The firestorm that killed 400 people in Hinckley, Minnesota, in 1894 included whirling towers of fire more than 200 feet high. Such firestorms are virtually impossible to extinguish.

Don't count on aerial flame retardant to save you from wildfire. Photo courtesy FEMA News Photo

Another possible symptom of a monster fire is the "pyrocumulus cloud." As the heating of the air goes on because of the fire, more and more moisture is being drawn up into the atmosphere and the cloud is formed. It has the same appearance as the "mushroom cloud" associated with a nuclear detonation because, indeed, the mushroom cloud is a pyrocumulus cloud. Lightning can form within such a cloud and subsequent cloud to ground lightning can start more fires. Since there is so much moisture involved in forming the cloud, it may produce rain, which could hurt the fire that created it.

Firestorms and fire whirls and the like are comparatively rare and only are possible when the fire is big enough. Wildfires are not rare at all. They're a perfectly natural occurrence, the means by which nature cleans out dead and dying vegetation, rejuvenating the land. When mankind interferes with this process, more devastating fires may result because more dead vegetation is on the ground, more dead trees are standing and, with too much forest density, flames can leap easily from tree to tree, not needing to work their way more slowly across the land to reach a fresh source of combustible materials.

Our Friend, The Sun

Many scientists agree that a major consideration in terms of radical climate change – pollution and other factors notwithstanding – is obviously the Sun. Elsewhere in this book, we discuss the potential difficulties arising due to solar flares and other phenomena originating from the Sun. But, the Sun, as we know, is cyclical as well. It is generally conceded that the Sun, as this is written, is approaching the "solar minimum" of the current 11-year cycle. The solar minimum, according to NASA, is best described as a period between solar maximums.

But the 11-year solar activity cycle is one thing, while the cyclical temperature variations of the Sun are something totally different. Much controversy has arisen concerning solar activity. Basically, when the Sun's surface is hotter, we are hotter; and, when the Sun's surface is not quite so hot, we are cooler. This may seem obvious, and it should be. This cycle of solar activity as regards temperature cannot be construed as being the same as the 11-year cycle, although logic suggests they are certainly interconnected. If the temperature cycle were only a period of 11 years, "normal" would be a meaningless word. Indeed, some scientists believe that our 21st century will usher in the next mini-ice age.

In the event of dramatically rising waters or advancing ice sheets, certain areas may become uninhabitable. Some food producing portions of the Northern Hemisphere would either be too sun-scorched to yield crops or be covered over by advancing glaciers. In regard to a "Mini Ice Age," which may well be linked to minimal sunspot activity, it should be remembered that the one which took place between 1645 and 1715, took a scant 10 years to develop. The story goes that Londoners were able to ride in their carriages on the frozen River Thames. The effects of global warming (except for engendering storms of greater intensity), whatever the causes, are considerably slower to mature. If the Earth is warming due to natural cycles or man's technology or both or neither, heat will become more and more of a concern as the warming cycle progresses. Heat waves – prolonged periods of higher than normal temperatures – can have a killing effect.

The NOAA (National Oceanic and Atmospheric Administration) Office of

Odd as it may seem, scientists generally agree that solar cycles can result in flooding.
Photo courtesy FEMA News Photo

Climate, Water and Weather Services offers some chilling figures (pardon the pun). Among weather-related causes, deaths from heat are second in any given year only to the effects of cold. Sometimes cold can't even compete. Take the heat wave of 1980, in which 1,250 people died. That figure was over seven times the number of persons killed in a typical year (175) by high temperatures and solar radiation. As the Weather Service points out, this figure of 175 people dying due to heat in a typical year only counts direct casualties. There is no way to calculate how many people succumb because excessive heat and humidity have exacerbated an already existing condition.

I often joke that Georgia did not invent humidity but merely perfected it. The combination of heat and humidity to make oppressive conditions, coupled with high ozone levels in and around large industrial centers and elsewhere, makes a lethal cocktail for persons with respiratory and heart conditions, and the for the very young and the very old. The very young, of course, are essentially helpless. The very old will, at times, be found passed out or expired from the heat when a perfectly serviceable air conditioning unit was present and merely had to be turned on. Perhaps the person forgot or was disoriented or never realized that body temperature was reaching dangerously high levels.

The National Weather Service (NWS) cannot change the weather, of course, but it can change how individuals and communities might be able to deal more effectively with extremely high temperatures. The NWS uses a heat index to tell you how hot it feels when the relative humidity is factored into the air temperature. Years ago, it was sometimes called the "discomfort index," and a more accurate name would be hard to imagine. If you have a Yahoo e-mail account, for example, and you go to "Weather," you will be given a graphic containing temperature and humidity for whatever specific geographic location you have selected. This graphic also shows you "Feels Like." That's the Heat Index.

An example employed by the National Weather Service uses a 96° Fahrenheit air temperature with a relative humidity of 65 percent. How hot that feels may surprise you – try 121° Fahrenheit! The Weather Service points out that these HI or heat indices were devised for exposure under shady conditions with a light wind to cool you. If you are in full sunshine, the temperature will feel 15 degrees warmer still. Factor in stronger winds and drier air and you can have even more "fun in the sun."

There is some sobering information concerning temperatures of 130° or higher. Heat stroke and sun stroke are likely with continued exposure. But you can get in trouble with prolonged exposure and physical activity with a heat index of only 80° to 90° F.

As this is written, we are in a solar minimum and the reduced sunspot activity is such that, at certain times, powerful telescopes can detect no sunspot activity whatsoever. This is normal. Some persons are concerned over the duration of the current solar minimum. Such concerns may or may not be groundless. In either event, mankind has absolutely no control over the forces of nature. We may be able to marginally influence things on our own Earth, but there is nothing we can do that in any way impacts solar activity. So, since we're about to enter a period of greater sunspot activity, we will have more solar flares, and we may have to deal with what the Sun dishes out after that, however unpleasant that might be. Get your sunscreen and keep it handy. And, don't forget the polarized sunglasses.

In the great scheme of things, considering our total lack of control over the Sun and what it does or does not do to our planet, contemplating the Sun is a good way to keep ourselves grounded.

Water, Water, Everywhere

However one sits on this side or that of the global warming debate, it is clear that the possibility exists not only for Katrina- and Andrew-like hurricanes to strike the USA mainland but that these larger and enormously destructive storms may hit with increased frequency and power. As I write this, three tropical storms are poised off the coasts of Florida and one of these storms appears to be shaping up as a possible textbook hurricane.

The El Nino effect can result in catastrophic flooding. Photo courtesy FEMA News Photo

Super storms, in turn, give rise to swarms of tornados and the one aspect of a hurricane that is even more deadly than its winds, the storm surge causing ruinous coastal flooding. As the post-Katrina conditions along the American Gulf Coast amply illustrated, the devastating effect of coastal flooding can endure for months or even years.

Often, in the course of a hurricane's destruction, there are torrential rains; yet abnormally high rainfall totals can occur without a hurricane's impetus. Whatever the cause, flash flooding can be devastating, turning ordinary streets and roads into deadly, swift coursing streams, washing away vehicles, wreaking destruction and death. Absent special coverage, most rising-water-related damage to structures is not even covered by insurance. Higher than average snowfall totals or quicker than normal spring thaws can swell existing streams and the rivers into which they feed, causing waterways to rise above flood stage

FEMA distributes sandbags in Fargo, North Dakota. Photo courtesy FEMA News Photo

There's a town underneath all that water: Oakville, Iowa, June 2008.
Photo courtesy FEMA Newes Photo

and overflow their banks, washing out fields and towns in their path along the flood plain.

But the concept of global warming carries with it much more than higher global temperatures and intensified storms. Whatever the reason, the polar icecaps are reducing in size. With the melt-off of cubic mile after cubic mile of fresh-water Arctic sea ice and Greenland glacier comes the very real potential for radical cooling of the British Isles and much of Western Europe, due to a slowdown or shutdown of the Gulf Stream.

The Gulf Stream is actually a two-way "street," part of which is called the North Atlantic Meridional Overturning Circulation – NAMOC, for short. The Gulf Stream brings warm waters up from the Caribbean, which allows England, Scotland, Wales, the Irelands and Western Europe to have temperate climates. This two-way street, however, can be closed for repairs when the temperature and salinity of the interchange location in the North Atlantic are altered. For the Gulf Stream to work and the warm current to come north, a returning current of salt water must travel back. An oversimplification, perhaps, but if traffic in one direction is reduced or stopped, traffic in both directions is affected. If the circulation is seriously altered, the British Isles and Western Europe will have drastically colder winters at best. At worst, the Northern Hemisphere could experience a return to glaciation and a new Ice Age – minus

The aftermath of Hurricane Ike. Photo courtesy FEMA News Photo

the cute animated animals. The ultimate irony would be that global warming – whatever the cause and extent – causes global cooling.

The End of the Mayan Calendar: December 21, 2012

I remember when President Kennedy was assassinated and everyone was speculating about all sorts of odd things about the terrible event. One popular pastime was to look for coincidences. For example, President Lincoln, also assassinated, had a vice-president named "Johnson," as did President Kennedy.

Well, and this admittedly sounds weird, when it comes to the date 12-21-2012, it could be expressed as 12-21-21-12 if we substituted for 20 the number 21, standing for the 21st century. And if we rearrange the date so that the day comes before the month, as in military dates, we get 21-12-21-12. Then, if we keep the regular civilian date order with the month of December expressed as

12 and 21 for the day and add month 12 of century 21, we have 12-21-12-21. We have created a palindrome! If we repeat it twice, we have a double palindrome!

My point is that we are surrounded by coincidences, not all of which are necessarily meaningful. Does my attempt at levity mean I don't take the End of the Mayan Calendar as a possible portent of bad things? Not necessarily. The Mayan calendar is based on various celestial cycles, including the planet Venus, the Earth's Moon and the Sun. The year 2012 will signal the end of an 11-year solar cycle, but on a precise date – December 21, 2012 – there will be a planetary alignment. The Mayan Long Count Calendar started in 3114 BC – more than five thousand years ago – and stops on December 21, 2012. Everything from planetary alignment to alignment with galactic center to massive solar flares to a polar shift are predicted by some to occur on that date. There are claims that decoding a segment of the Torah has predicted and accurately chronicled various events and that this may predict a Near Earth Object impacting our planet in 2012.

Humankind seems to thrive on excitement and positively craves predicting the future. "The End of The World" has been heralded many times before and, if we survive this one, will doubtlessly be touted many times again. As this is written, books have already appeared about 2012 and movies are scheduled. As December 21, 2012 approaches, interest will intensify and, I daresay, rival and even surpass the frenzy that was associated with Y2K. There will almost certainly be panic buying and hoarding of everything from Coleman fuel to canned goods to cartridges – and not the kind filled with ink.

The problem is, you might think, that if December 21, 2012 does prove to be the end of the world, what good will extra supplies be? And you'd be right. But, if it isn't the end of time – at least for the population of planet Earth – there may still be a great deal of last-minute panic. People are going to want to put away more than bread and milk. Many of them may want to put away what *you've* got because they never heeded any information concerning the possibilities for 2012.

If, in fact, as December 21, 2012 approaches, scientists note any oddities giving support to the possibility for calamity, there could be widespread panic. As some contend, if the governments of the world learned that there really was something to the Mayan Long Count Calendar ending on December 21, 2012, would they tell us? There's a good chance such information would be withheld; it would not be "spilled" until some amateur astronomer realized something anomalous was shaping up. Amateurs account for many of the greatest astronomical discoveries. If it were realized that world governments were withholding information about impending doom, it is highly likely all semblance of order would vanish. Even if we are to die as Earth is destroyed, wouldn't we rather greet death in some other guise other than that of a howling mob?

Add to the Mayan Long Count Calendar and the interpretation of the I Ching the most widely held beliefs about the Ends of Days as derived from the Bible, most particularly The Book of Revelations, and the next few years could be a doozy. I claim no expertise as relates to Biblical matters and prophecy in particular; but the Four Horsemen of The Apocalypse sure seem to be saddled up and ready to ride, don't they?

"The Bomb"

We don't need the Mayan calendar to end to obliterate much of Earth's population, of course, because we can achieve the same effect ourselves by having a significant number of thermonuclear detonations. If radical anti-western forces such as al-Qaida get hold of nuclear weapons – perhaps the ones in Pakistan

The deadliest mushroom of all. Photo courtesy FEMA News Photo

or those rumored to be available on the international black market – they will use those weapons. During the Cold War with the then-Soviet Union – which we might someday look back upon as the good old days – there was the policy known by the acronym MAD, standing for "Mutually Assured Destruction." In those days, as many readers may recall, despite the fact that the Soviet Union was, as Ronald Reagan aptly described it, "the evil empire," no one ever thought that the leaders of Communist Russia embraced making it big in the afterlife as their greatest goal. The true zealots of al-Qaida and other organizations of their ilk look forward to being rewarded after death for what normal people would consider heinously despicable acts. If they get nukes, they will use them and all of us will have to live with the consequences – or die because of them.

When I was growing up in Chicago and attending public schools in the 1950s, we held air raid drills, and we actually practiced "duck and cover." I lived about four and one-half miles west and seven and one-half miles south of the Chicago Loop, which would likely have been Ground Zero. All that our "duck and cover" drills would have achieved, even under optimal conditions, would have been keeping all our little student-shaped piles of ash more neatly organized than they would have been otherwise.

A small nuclear device launched into the atmosphere atop a pretty basic guided missile can do a great deal more damage than mass casualties and property destruction. A high-altitude detonation of a nuclear device can also be used to create an electromagnetic pulse, or EMP. The acronym for this type of EMP is "HEMP," standing for High-altitude ElectroMagnetic Pulse. Basically, electrical and magnetic fields are created during the detonation, which disrupt electrical/electronic systems such as your computer, the computer in your car, and the electronics in a satellite. Military hardware is "hardened" to resist HEMP. The older tube technology, which was prevalent in certain Soviet-era Russian aircraft, was less sensitive to permanent damage; the tubes could easily be replaced. More sophisticated electronic or electrical devices, however, – including the power grid – get fried. The effect is gradual, occurring over weeks or months. However, another meaning of the acronym "HEMP" is Hydrodynamic Electromagnetic Pulse. Deriving what information one can from the field of astrophysics, the hydrodynamic bounce to which this term apparently refers might greatly accelerate the effectiveness of an EMP, thus further complicating fortifying electrical and electronic systems against it.

The weapon used to create an EMP can be anything from 10 megatons and up, and there are a variety of detonation altitudes depending on the size of the weapon and the desired geographic coverage. The result of a well-designed EMP could be to reduce us to the daily living conditions of the late nineteenth century. This would not be a vacation.

Terrorist Attacks

Nature targets its destruction randomly, but terrorists will kill whomever is unfortunate enough to be present at their target, and that target is chosen

No explanation necessary. Ground Zero, 2001. Photo courtesy FEMA News Photo

deliberately. We should never forget the multiple attacks that comprised the Mumbai massacre that began on November 26, 2008, and finally ended on November 29 and cost the lives of over 170 innocent people. On July 11, 2006, there were seven terrorist bombings in Mumbai within a scant 11 minutes. Two hundred and nine people were killed and there were three and one-half times as many persons injured. The number of casualties could easily have numbered into the thousands.

Terrorism is a fact of life in the modern world and will likely remain so for generations to come. The use of chemical and/or biological agents for mass killing is problematic, because of the difficulties of dissemination. In the immediate aftermath of the September 11 attacks, there was considerable concern over crop dusters – namely, that these small aircraft, which are used for chemical overspraying of farmers' fields, could be used to release harmful substances over American cities and towns. The more likely terrorist tool for indiscriminate mass killing, however, is the nuclear device. Everyone thinks in terms of nuclear detonations or conventional explosives being used to disseminate nuclear contaminants – the "dirty bomb." A study more than two decades ago, as I recall, suggested other means by which nuclear material could be used against an urban population, one of the most insidious ways involving no greater technology than a dripping water spigot and an open window. It was posited that a radioactive substance could be placed in an uncovered container on the sill of an open window. Water would be rigged to drip onto the radioactive material, the water becoming contaminated, the irradiated water evaporating into the air and lots of people starting to get really sick. How well such a technique might work is something that I hope we never find out.

More conventionally, terrorists like blowing things up, which tends to hurtle lots of shrapnel into the unsuspecting persons near the explosion. Often, the bad guys blow themselves up, again hearkening back to being rewarded for the death toll they've chalked up by lots of perks in the afterlife. There isn't a terrorist worth his salt who wouldn't drool over the opportunity to detonate a nuclear weapon, but such devices are usually too large and too heavy to be carried about nonchalantly until the moment of detonation, and the level of sophistication required to construct even the most primitive atomic bomb is well beyond the usual sort of person who would strap an explosives vest to his body.

Conventional explosives are the more likely tools; the old C-4, the more modern Semtex and similar "plastiques" are better suited to mass murderer wannabees blowing up delivery trucks and passenger cars loaded with nails and wire, using gasoline as an accelerant or attempting a genuine fuel-air bomb effect. A fuel-air bomb, or thermobaric weapon, is almost as destructive as a small nuclear device but leaves no "unsightly residue." Utilizing the oxygen in the air, a fuel air bomb literally ignites that oxygen rather than carrying its own oxidizer. If you can get around the unpredictability of the weather, such bombs can be extraordinarily efficient for wiping something totally off the map. Enclosed structures that are heavily fortified with concrete even serve to magnify the explosive force of the weapon. A side effect is that with the oxygen consumed, no matter what other precautions persons unfortunate enough to be in the area of the explosion might take, victims will suffocate because there is no oxygen left to breathe.

Multiple comparatively small terrorist attacks, like those experienced so often in the Middle East, whether involving homicide/suicide bombings, roadside improvised explosives devices (IEDs), drive-by shootings or random attacks on restaurants and stores could have a devastating effect going well beyond the actual incidents themselves, precipitating economic disruptions, retaliatory attacks against supposed or alleged terrorist sympathizers, or other effects not so immediate. Such an attack would cause a significant tear in the social fabric.

We do not have to imagine what it would be like with an armed lunatic

The Pentagon, post-9/11/01. Photo courtesy FEMA News Photo

or lunatics going on what the media loves to call a "shooting spree" in a shopping center or a school. Such has already happened and – God forbid – will quite possibly happen again. To a terrorist or a madman – the terms can be interchangeable – large numbers of people, likely unarmed, are irresistible as a target.

Think about it for a moment. Do you see security personnel who patrol your favorite mall carrying anything more than a chemical spray or a Taser? What good will either of those do if a crazed killer enters that mall heavily armed? Not a thing. The nomenclature appropriate to this situation is "soft target." Okay, maybe there's an off-duty cop and maybe he or she is armed. But maybe not. Maybe there are a few legally armed private citizens. But maybe they left their firearms locked in their cars. At best, you're talking about one or a few small, concealable handguns against an assault rifle and other possible weapons. During the Mumbai massacre, weaponless security guards – India has very strict weapons policies for security guards – had to take cover like everybody else, because they had no means with which to respond to the attackers. And, in India, virtually nobody else is armed, except for police and military. And the bad guys, of course.

Clearly, the supposed political incorrectness and possible liability issues associated with security personnel carrying firearms has prepped public facilities all across America as targets-in-waiting. Without a change in attitude, they will remain such. Be alert to your surroundings and don't think for a moment that the presence of a guy in a uniform with a pepper spray on his hip – no matter how well-intended and brave that individual may be – will deter someone who is not only perfectly willing to die, but may actualy wish to die, from trying to kill you and your family.

The mundane, taken to the extreme, can be just as threatening. In the winter, there can be ice storms, heavier-than-normal snowfalls, and blizzards. In the summertime, there can be heat emergencies, wherein protracted triple digit temperatures can precipitate sickness and even death. Tornados can wreak havoc. Whether ice storm or heat wave, electrical power is critical to us all. The sheer weight of ice on power lines themselves or overhanging tree limbs can tear down power lines. High heat levels, especially over a protracted period of time, will place levels of strain on the power grid that cannot be sustained indefinitely. Rolling blackouts can occur. If the proper course of action is not followed at the appropriate time, damage can be done to components of the grid, damage which is neither easily nor quickly fixable.

Toxic chemical spills and fires near where you work, the release of noxious elements into the air your kids may be breathing at school, localized outbreaks of seriously contagious diseases, even an interruption in the pipelines that deliver fuel for our automobiles or natural gas to power our cooking stoves, heat our homes or turn the turbines which generate our electricity – all of this can alter your life.

Are you ready to deal with this?

Are you ready to survive?

CHAPTER 2:
LEVELS OF
PREPAREDNESS

September is National Preparedness Month, during which businesses, private groups, and state and federal governments unite to stress the importance of preparedness for natural and manmade disasters. Georgia, where I live, has a website dedicated to disaster preparedness (www.ready.ga.gov). Check out your own state's preparations. If you were to examine how the United States government breaks down disaster planning for popular consumption, you would discover that there are three classifications: America, Business and Kids. This is a good breakdown, pushing the idea of planning, being informed and looking at preparation for disaster with a positive, pro-active mental attitude.

Ahern with some typical gear to have around for a wide range of emergency use. At left, a wet dry vacuum cleaner, at right an aluminum step ladder, at right foreground a cooler that can be loaded with ice. Ahern holds a water container.

The breakdown in these pages goes quite a bit further, however, trying to view American life in its principal components and tweaking preparation from this perspective. Therefore, we'll discuss survival preparedness in terms of the individual; the nuclear family; and the extended family, in that order.

My own situation is a bit unique. My wife and I are almost invariably together 24/7/365 – and we actually love it. As this is written, our children and their families live either 15 minutes to the north or 20 minutes to the south. Our friends are spread all over the USA, few living near us. For the bulk of my life, my office has been at home, as it is now. But the typical American works outside the home. His nuclear family is reunited most evenings; his extended family is reunited on holidays and for reunion-like functions (weddings, funerals, actual reunions); his family-like friends are geographically close, for the most part. His business is a place where he (or she) goes alone or in company (car pooling or public transportation) five days a week.

Because the individual drifts in and out of group settings in the normal course of events, in a situation with absolutely no forewarning at all, odds are significant that the individual may well be separated from his or her nuclear family, extended family, business organization or localized prepared community. The individual's first order of business, after seeing to his immediate personal well-being, is to connect with the most basic of his or her groups.

Let's consider two separate disaster scenarios. As I am writing this, a hurricane is tearing across the Caribbean. However strong it finally becomes, however much damage it will cause, however many lives it may impact or cause to be lost, cannot be foretold; but, at least persons in the storm's projected path have time to prepare, perhaps even to evacuate. Then again, the storm may fizzle out and turn into a non-event. The individual, in this sort of situation where there is advanced warning and at least a modest amount of preparation time, will almost certainly link up with his or her nuclear family and possibly with the larger groups. If evacuation will not be an element of this individual's game plan for getting through the disaster, and if a local prepared community organization exists, the individual will quite likely find himself not functioning as a solitary individual at all, but rather functioning within a pre-established or ad hoc group. Time is required, in the majority of cases, for most action beyond the individual level, certainly beyond the nuclear family level.

The second disaster scenario provides no true warning at all. Again, as I am writing this, a Latin American nation is dealing with the immediate aftermath of an exceedingly powerful earthquake which has, so far, claimed the lives of 500 persons. The earthquake happened as earthquakes do: everything is normal, but a split second later, the ground shakes and buildings collapse around you.

Both a hurricane and an earthquake, although their after-effects are of long duration, begin and end comparatively quickly. The hurricane may batter a coastal area with high winds and high tides, beach erosion and flooding for a few days before the storm surge rises and the hurricane actually hits, the storm itself usually passing on in a matter of hours. Earthquakes are positively ephemeral, the actual shaking typically lasting for less than a minute. There are aftershocks, of course, often nearly as severe as the actual earthquake itself.

In the cases of both of these natural disasters, disruption of basic services is a given, hardships multiplying and multiplying despite relief efforts. People run out of food and drinkable water. Medical facilities are stretched beyond endurance and law enforcement is all but crushed beneath the disaster's sheer weight. And in both scenarios, electricity is knocked out. The interruption of electrical power is a disaster which grows and grows and doesn't stop growing until power is restored. As the crisis drags on, things only become worse and worse.

Consider this scenario. There is sabotage by a person or persons unknown of a significant portion of the power grid. You're on your way home during the rush hour and the traffic lights stop functioning; you're in gridlock, alone in your automobile. There was no advance warning. Cellular communications are a mess; one of the radio stations has its backup generator working and you learn that traffic is at an almost total stop everywhere between you and your family. After two hours of covering less than a mile, you are running out of gas. Gas stations you've passed are closed, of course, because there is no electricity to run the pumps or the cash registers. You notice that a growing number of cars are being left in the road where they ran out of gas, making travel even more problematic. Soon, the car which you are driving will have to be abandoned as well. Although you usually carry an extra gallon of gas in an approved container in the trunk of your car, you're not driving your car, but your wife's car instead because she took your car in for an oil change. Your individual survival kit is in your car as well, but your wife's kit is in this car and the contents are much the same.

When you finally have to abandon the car, knowing it will be looted before you can retrieve it, all you have with you to get to your home is what was stashed in the car and what you normally carry on your person. There are miles to go before you can reach home, unite with your nuclear family, and perhaps interact with larger groups. So you walk, worried about your family, knowing that they are concerned for your safety as well.

Cellular communications, that great bastion of 21st-century existence, are for the most part trashed. But you own a laptop and, before you abandoned your wife's car, you're able to get online. It seems as though this power failure is all up and down the coast and there are unconfirmed reports of more blackouts elsewhere in the country. It's starting to get dark. As you keep walking, you notice three guys who appear to be breaking into an ATM. You quicken your pace. You may have just heard a string of shots.

Your nightmare is just beginning. As an individual, your greatest goal is to reunite with your nuclear family and be about the business of getting through this.

In the case of the Category 4 or 5 hurricane, there may have been days of advance warning. The earthquake's occurrence may have been strongly suspected by seismologists; but, at the current level of technology, exactitude is impossible, so prediction beyond a general caution or advisory is also impossible. Essentially, an earthquake strikes without warning. The fictional terrorist-related rolling blackout might have been suspected by Homeland Security, the various intelligence agencies or the FBI; but, beyond raising the alert status to a different color or level – which would be predicated only upon the strongest possible inferences of an impending attack – there is nothing else to do except to go on with daily life as usual. With each day that passes without a major terrorist incident, the possibility of an attack gets pushed further and further away from conscious awareness. Each time you "dodge a bullet" and the killer natural disaster doesn't directly impact you, it becomes easier and easier to indulge in self-delusion and to act as if you are somehow immune.

You must be aware. No one is immune.

In the Workplace

Consider your business life. You spend 40 hours per week or more interacting with persons at your office or factory or store. There are 168 hours in a week. That means you spend a little less than 25 percent of every week with your work-related colleagues. Translated into probability that you'll be at work in the event of a natural or manmade disaster, you have a roughly one in four chance of being on the job when whatever it is goes down.

If no one else at your place of business has taken steps to do so, you need to get things organized – even if it means being stuck with added responsibility without any additional compensation. Get together with whoever is in charge and determine what plans may or may not already exist. Make certain that the ownership doesn't view such preparedness planning as interfering with their daily business. You may have to do a little selling of the idea to get things started. But you have this book. You have access to all the information the United States government provides via the internet. You have immediate resources available from the police department, the fire department, and other civil-service organizations. Whoever underwrites your firm's insurance may well be able to provide additional resources for safety education.

Organize the people you work with so that each has a specific responsibility in the overall plan for your business. Obviously, your place of business will have a first aid kit or kits and at least a few extinguishers. Make certain that everyone knows how to use them. In most areas, business fire extinguishers will be checked and tagged each year. No such program exists for first aid kits in small businesses, however. Make certain that the items in the First Aid kit or kits are replenished as needed and that other items that may be too old to be effective are replaced on a regularly-scheduled basis.

Have emergency plans. Check all emergency exits, making certain that they are clearly marked and never blocked. If you work in an upper floor of a high rise building, determine whether or not fire department ladders will be tall enough to reach your floor. If not, pre-planned exit strategies – to include both gear and technique – must be created. You can consult with your local fire department to know how high their ladders will reach. The usual boundaries are no less than three and no more than seven floors up. If you're on the eighth floor, you won't have a lot of choices.

As an aside, remember about fire ladder heights when you take a room in a hotel. A few years before September 11, I had the occasion to spend the night in one of the hotels brought down during the September 11 attack on the World Trade Center. Brings all sorts of thoughts to mind.

A manufacturing business we owned some years back employed more than a half-dozen people. There were several other buildings nearby, and it turned out that one of them contained a meth lab. We were in our building when we realized that heavily armed men were running from along the front end of our building. Immediately, I gathered together our employees and rushed them to the windowless room on the far end of the building and we waited. As it turned out, the heavily armed men in work and casual clothes were narcotics officers and they were closing in on that meth lab with a surprise raid. There was no way we could have anticipated something like that taking place. Moving the employees to safety was purely spur of the moment.

But so many other situations can be planned for.

Lay in an emergency water supply and some emergency foods that can be rotated out periodically. Make certain to have a working emergency radio. Establish policies concerning business closures. A firm I worked for when I was in my early twenties had three facilities in the metropolitan Chicago area. I managed one that was located in a far northern suburb. The overall manager of all three facilities was out of town on business when a severe civil dislocation erupted. The man running the facility in the Chicago Loop called me and asked my opinion on whether or not he should close and send people home for their own safety. There was no established procedure for him to consult and follow.

Businesses must have emergency procedures established to meet with likely contingencies. In what part of your building will personnel take shelter in the event of a tornado warning? If medical help is needed and cannot come to you, how close is the nearest facility to which you can bring someone? An old friend who specializes in security related matters discourages any businesses with which he deals from establishing themselves near a rail line. There's always the risk of sabotage and the even greater risk of an accident that can result in a chemical spill or noxious fumes being released. Trains moving quickly along a track can delay a fire truck or an ambulance when time is of the essence in an emergency.

Be prepared – at all levels!

CHAPTER 3:
INDIVIDUAL SURVIVAL PREPAREDNESS

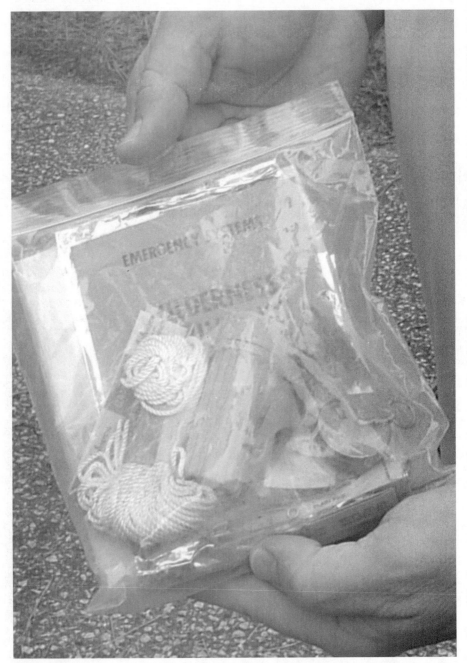

Miscellaneous survival gear, some of which Ahern has had for over 30 years – but it still works.

Mental attitude, of course, may not be everything, but without a positive mental attitude, miraculous intervention is all that will save you.

Assuming, then, that you believe in yourself and are motivated to do whatever is possible to achieve your goal, there are basic equipment issues to consider. No adult, except in areas where it is legally impermissible, should ever be without a **folding knife**, preferably one with a locking main blade, but a knife nonetheless. Even a small Swiss Army knife on a key ring is better than no knife at all. A stout lockblade folding hunter is the ideal. In areas where legal, certain of the automatic knives can be highly recommended. For example, the **Benchmade Model 9050** is an automatic knife, fitted with a safety lockout, so well-made and reliable that it is issued to certain United States military personnel. It is available with a standard or combo edge, such an arrangement consisting of a conventional edge for the leading half of the blade and serrations for the rearmost segment. Serrations, if they are done properly, make tasks like cutting cord, tubing or heavy fabric or other materials faster and easier. If well-designed, serrated edges can even be touched up when the standard portion of the blade is sharpened. A reliable knife is not going to be cheap, in either sense of the word. A knife without proper heat treat for holding an edge or with an unreliable lock that lets the blade pass the full-open position unintentionally when pressure is applied is an accident waiting to happen.

Custom knife makers are an option, of course, but many of the production knife companies offer excellent product. **Benchmade, Buck, Cold Steel, Pumawerke, Gerber, Al Mar, Lone Wolf** and several others come to mind

A perfect folding knife for the survival kit right down to its orange handle scales, this Benchmade model is made especially for use in water related environments but is just as good on land.

from good personal experience. There are more fine brands as well. For a good overview, visit a quality cutlery shop or a well-stocked gun store; or check out **A.G. Russell** (www.agrussell.com), either online or by ordering a catalog. Obtain a handy to use knife sharpener and, if you don't know how to use it, get someone who does know how to sharpen a knife to show you. Keep your knife sharp, as it will be safer and more reliable.

There are other items of basic personal equipment that should be available to you at all times. A functioning **cellular telephone** with a well-charged battery is an absolute necessity that can make the difference between life and death for yourself or anyone with you. Quick re-chargers, or the kind that can be run off the cigar lighter connection in an automobile, are handy in the extreme and should be kept available. For the most part, however, your battery will have a longer service life and hold its charge better if standard overnight-style **chargers** are used most of the time (my son, who uses a cellular phone a great deal, shared this bit of wisdom with me and it really works).

So you don't have to keep using cellular phone battery power to check the time or how much time has elapsed, make certain to wear a **dependable watch**. For my money, the most practical kind of watch is the kind that used to be called "self-winding," no battery required. If a watch such as this is too expensive or you have to have a whole bunch of other watch functions besides time and possibly the date, then get a good quality watch from a maker like Timex or Seiko or acquire what has become known as a "tactical wristwatch," a wristwatch designed for military and law enforcement use under harsh conditions. These wristwatches are good-sized, have various functions and look re-

Ahern uses exactly two wristwatches – at left a Timex, at right his vintage Rolex Sea Dweller.

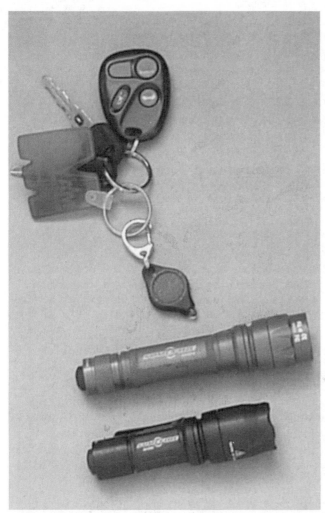

ally cool on a guy's wrist. One the best of this style timepiece is the **MTM Special Ops** (www.specialopswatch.com). Keep track of anticipated battery life for the watch and change out the battery at least a month before it is likely to start dying out.

A keyring-sized **LED light**, such as those from **Photon Micro-Light** (www.photonlight.com), should be on your ring. Choose the blue or white lights, as they are visible at great distances. Aside from being a terrific assist in a wide range of normal circumstances, for emergency lighting or signaling – a potentially vital feature – these economical little lights are a must.

Three of Ahern's favorite lights are this key ring Photon Freedom Micro-Light, the SureFire L-4 digital Lumamax and the small SureFire Backup.

Always carry **identification**. If you are a casualty, ID will assist rescue or recovery personnel with contacting your family to let them know your condition. It can also help to prove that you are one of the victims instead of one of the perpetrators.

Always carry at least some **cash**. In a crisis, remember that if the electricity goes down, ATMs and credit card swipers will not work and you'll be without financial resources. A good friend of mine always carries ten $100 bills neatly pressed within his wallet and a reasonable number of $20 bills in his pocket. The thousand dollars might be a bit extreme, but the idea behind it is sound. If supplies are short and you must pay scalpers' prices for necessities like milk or

Blackhawk! Warrior Wear Black Ops Boots are quick to put on and water and oil resistant. Boots like these or a pair of well worn track shoes, such as these New Balance 608s – with the right socks – are just what you need.

bread or even gasoline or propane, no one is going to want to take a check.

Wear **shoes** with which you can comfortably walk a good distance, if you must. For women especially, this is important, as so many women's shoes are built for looks rather than comfort. The solution is obvious for either sex, however: have a pair of **cushion-sole athletic socks** along with a pair of well-broken-in cross-trainers or hiking boots stashed in likely locations to be changed into if required. By likely locations, I mean your automobile, your desk or workstation or any other area where you might spend a great deal of time away from home.

With the exception of the track shoes – and you might be wearing such shoes or hiking boots to begin with, anyway – all of the items mentioned so far are normal, everyday things which would be kept on your person in the regular course of events, even if one were not concerned with disaster preparedness.

What you also need is an **individual kit**, and here is what I suggest that it contain:

There should be a spare, **charged battery** for your cellular telephone. It is assumed that you will have some sort of overnight AC outlet battery charger available at your home or office, but you may also have a **fast charger** for emergency use. Here, in the individual kit, is where that DC automobile charger can be a lifesaver.

A great many people always keep an individual-size **bottle of water** handy. Make certain that there is an extra one kept with your kit. Aside from drinking, clean water can be useful for bathing a wound or flushing debris from the eyes.

This Radio Shack emergency radio is inexpensive and reliable and automatically runs on batteries when the power goes.

This Midland radio runs on AC or DC or batteries and has a dynamo so the batteries can be hand-charged.

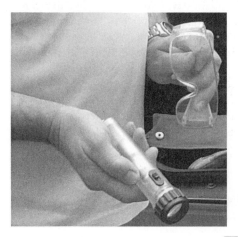

A small **AM/FM radio** is an absolute must in order to receive emergency broadcasts. Several compact, magneto-driven wind-up models are available these days, and they have sufficient range for most uses. Battery-operated models are also a good choice, provided you carry several extra **long-life batteries** in your kit.

To be assured of being able to see what you are doing and to have the mental comfort which holding off the darkness can provide, you'll want a **reliable light source** throwing a larger beam than what you'll keep on your key ring. Although the tactical lights are excellent for temporarily disrupting the vision of an attacker, be certain to acquire a light which also has lower-intensity capabilities. The "high beam" tends to burn through batteries and bulbs too rapidly for what might prove a protracted period of time. A flashlight that operates with a light-emitting diode will last and last. The inexpensive flashlights that must be shaken before being actuated and claim permanent battery power, in my personal experience with two examples, have proven to work quite well, although the beam is a little weak. They seem to be a good value. If you cannot locate one of these or one of the diode lights, or merely want something more conventional, find a name brand AA cell pocket flashlight. The **MagLite** (www. maglite.com) flashlights are outstanding and, with **Duracell** batteries, will last a very long time.

This little flashlight was advertised on television as never needing batteries. Just shake it and use it – it really works! Ahern has safety glasses in his left hand.

You'll want a **compass**. The GI style lensatic compasses are terrific and rugged, but an ordinary compass that can be acquired in a camping and outdoors store – even the kind that can be clipped onto a zipper pull – will work for the simplified type of land navigation required here, too, as long as you do your part and learn how to use a compass for basic land navigation. You are not going to have to prepare a dissertation on the difference between Magnetic North, True North and Grid North, but you will want to know the fundamentals of compass operation (see Chapter 20), along with the compass's limitations (such as proximity to steel objects, magnetism, etc.).

To go with your compass, you'll want a **local area map**. In major cities, a detailed and up-to-date street map could prove invaluable. Take the trouble to try a few land navigation exercises – make it a nuclear family project – so that you will thoroughly understand the instrument and have enough familiarity with the local area map(s) so there won't be any initial confusion.

A small, personal-sized **First Aid kit** needs to be part of your kit. I'm referring to the pocket sized ones, usually found in plastic snap closure boxes, typically containing various adhesive bandage sizes, burn cream, antiseptic wipes, and other basic supplies. Anyone with special medical requirements – perhaps an asthmatic who might require a fast acting inhaler – must make certain that such additional equipment is also included.

Three feet or so of **flexible plastic tubing**, the kind that is about a quarter-inch in diameter, is a must. If you are trapped beneath rubble or aiding someone who is, such a piece of tubing could literally make the difference between drawing a breath and suffocation. The tubing can be used as an emergency tourniquet – although tourniquets are not something an amateur should monkey with unless it's clearly a matter of life or immediate death – or can be used in other medical applications. The tubing is nothing more than a long, flexible straw, so it can be used to siphon gasoline, etc.

The better arrangement, should you need to siphon gas, is to go to an auto parts store like Auto Zone and get a **Victor siphon pump**. The squeezable diaphragm included with the siphon pump's tubing could prove very useful if you do have to siphon gasoline, because the only way to evacuate the air from an ordinary tube is to draw it out by mouth and gasoline not only is reported to taste bad, but it's bad for you – "bad" as in "toxic."

Am I telling you to steal gasoline from an abandoned vehicle if you must? Let your conscience be your guide, if the vehicle is truly abandoned and you are in a life or death situation. More to the point, you may have gasoline in your lawn tractor or lawn mower, gasoline in a second car, etc., and using a siphon can allow you to fill up the tank of the car you might be using for evacuation, rather than leaving precious gasoline behind.

Disposable dust masks are easily found in a wide range of stores, and they are quite inexpensive. They come in packages holding several each. One such package should be a part of your kit. Masks such as these will not take the place of a respirator or the more sophisticated rubberized plastic masks with replaceable dust filters, such as those from 3M, but they can help. In a disas-

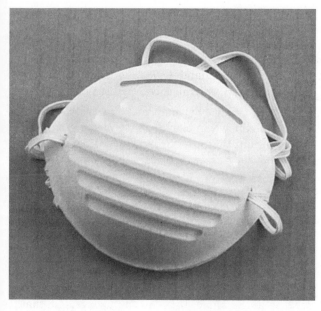

ter situation, your body will be under stress and require greater amounts of oxygen than normally needed; being able to filter out concrete dust or other airborne pollutants, even to a minor degree, could prove invaluable.

These commonly available dust masks are inexpensive, yet can filter out dust and other particulate matter to help keep your respiratory system clear.

Each kit should have a **multi-tool**. Think of multi-tools as a Swiss Army Knife on steroids. The Swiss Army Knife people (**Victorinox** and **Wenger**) even make a multi-tool, as does **Gerber/Fiskars**, as does **Sheffield**, as does the originator of the multi-tool concept, **Leatherman Tool Group**. These tools can be had with various types of pliers, files, knife blades, and other goodies, their

principal advantage over a Swiss Army Knife being their larger size (easier to hold and capable of taking on more robust tasks) and the pliers. Some models even incorporate locking pliers. And, of course, all the tools fold into the handles and the entire unit, when closed, is barely larger than a good-sized lockblade folding knife.

Ahern's main key ring has a screwdriver with a full size head and a Swiss-Tech tool incorporating pliers and two different screwdrivers – and it really works.

If you need **glasses** in order to read, to prevent eyestrain or just for seeing (contacts can become lost, dry out under dusty conditions, etc.), your chances of survival will be greatly reduced if your eyewear is lost or broken. Having multiple pairs of prescription eyeglasses can be burdensomely expensive. The solution (for many vision types) is the economical reading glasses which can be acquired at the local pharmacy, at Wal-Mart and similar stores. I've normally seen these priced around $10 or $12 a pair. They may not be perfect for your vision requirements, but if they will allow you to afford several spare pairs of glasses, including a pair for your kit, they are worth your consideration. I always keep a pair of these economical glasses in my car – just in case.

The physical requirements of a survival situation cannot be overestimated. The demands on your body may be unlike anything you may have experienced.

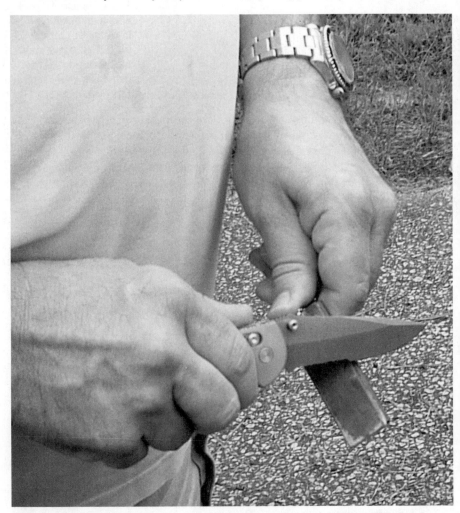

Ahern prepares to shave a magnesium stick to assist in fire starting. This one is particularly handy because it features a chain that enables it to attach to other gear.

And, your body will be pumping adrenalin, as well. The means by which to keep your blood sugar at close-to-normal levels and simply to satisfy hunger during and after exertion can prove vital to your continued well being. A modest amount of **high-energy food bars** should be part of every kit.

Just as individual medical equipment might be needed, so certainly also will regularly self-administered **medications** be important. A week's or ten days' supply should be made part of your kit. If you are supposed to take an aspirin every day or a Lipitor or blood pressure medication, etc., in a stress situation your meds will be needed all the more.

A folded plastic **raincoat**, preferably with a hood, is useful in the kit. The plastic raincoat can provide protection from dust, insulate the body against cold and serve a variety of other purposes as a field expedient. A large, heavy

Ultimate Survival Kit with chain-type hand saw and Blast Match for emergency fire starting.

duty (not lawn and leaf type) **plastic bag** can serve as everything from a tube shelter to a means for carrying supplies. Have one along.

I haven't smoked in a number of years, but there's always a disposable cigarette **lighter** handy and one belongs in your kit. The ability to start a fire simply and easily can be of inestimable importance. Certainly, a trained survival expert can make a magnifying lens out of ice and use that to focus sunlight and start a fire, but the average person cannot do that and there might not be any ice around anyway. The lighter is faster and easier. The flame can also be used to sterilize the tweezers that should also be included in your kit (Swiss Army Knives usually have tweezers), useful for removing splinters, pieces of glass, etc. A **magnifying glass**, when not used to start fires, can prove very valuable to aid in finding small pieces of glass or debris on the skin or, worse, in the eyes.

The "space"-type **blankets**, are offered from various sources, including the Kennedy Space Center. I got mine, along with a sleeping bag version of the same material, from Maine Military Supply (www.mainemilitary.com). The blankets and sleeping bags are pocket-sized and can be used for everything from making a shelter to wrapping up in one for warmth or protection from the sun to signaling aircraft because they are reflective. They reflect 90 percent of body heat back to the user and they are quite inexpensive.

Iodine tablets to protect your thyroid in the event of a radiation incident and **salt tablets** to replace what you will sweat out if serious exertion is required will round out the typical kit's expendables. Check with your doctor on both of these.

And don't forget a roll of **duct tape**, which has so many potential uses in a survival scenario that just listing them would require – and has required – a separate book.

But expendables are also time sensitive. Your kit must be monitored on a regular schedule. Three-year-old flashlight batteries may be at the end of their shelf life and year-old prescription medications might not only prove ineffective for their intended purpose, but possibly dangerous to consume. The simplest way is to determine a safe cushion for medications, food stuffs and the like and mark these changeover dates on a calendar, just like a woman will keep track of her monthly cycle or a householder will keep tabs on when to change furnace/air conditioner filters. If this is done, prescription medications will not be wasted because of expiration. If you live in an area prone to extremes of temperature, this, too, must be taken into account, not just for the meds, but for batteries, as well.

A part of your kit that is usually neglected can prove vital: a **listing of individuals' names and telephone numbers** (don't rely on what's in your cellular telephone alone) and key persons (your cardiologist, your daughter's Girl Scout leader, etc.) and institutions (your children's schools, the bowling alley where a family member plays once a week, etc.) as well as agent names, policy numbers and contact information for all insurance policies. If you have any special medical conditions, allergies or other considerations which could impact emergency care, you might elect to wear a **medic alert bracelet** or medallion.

Although the items in your kit are numerous, the actual size of the kit is comparatively small if packed properly, most items taking up very little room. And, spare room in the housing for your kit can be filled up with more water, more energy bars, etc.

The kit should be as near to you as possible at all times. This implies that your kit should be easily portable. What this may also mean is that you might need to have more than one kit. Ideally, your kit should be so close by that you can get to it in minutes or less from the realization of an emergency.

If you are an office worker or a construction worker, let's say, the kit should be in your car that is parked close by to your work site. If you ride share often, you could keep your kit in a briefcase or backpack and carry it with you. More likely, you'll take your chances when ride sharing and have a second kit in your office. But here's a better idea. If you are into organized ride sharing with like-minded individuals, stashing your spare kit in the trunk of your ride's car should be perfectly acceptable and is much safer than running the risk of being caught without a kit in an emergency. If you use a plan where your spare kit goes from vehicle to vehicle, make certain that all of the ride sharers have a key that will afford access to the car in the event that the principal operator of the vehicle is a casualty.

As part of basic preparation, stay informed concerning current events, have access to breaking news while on the job, if possible, and have pre-set standards which, once they are met, trigger an appropriate emergency response. Then go with your gut.

CHAPTER 4:
NUCLEAR FAMILY PREPAREDNESS

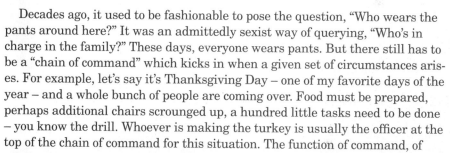

Decades ago, it used to be fashionable to pose the question, "Who wears the pants around here?" It was an admittedly sexist way of querying, "Who's in charge in the family?" These days, everyone wears pants. But there still has to be a "chain of command" which kicks in when a given set of circumstances arises. For example, let's say it's Thanksgiving Day – one of my favorite days of the year – and a whole bunch of people are coming over. Food must be prepared, perhaps additional chairs scrounged up, a hundred little tasks need to be done – you know the drill. Whoever is making the turkey is usually the officer at the top of the chain of command for this situation. The function of command, of course, is the delegation of authority:

"You – make those mashed potatoes! You and you – set that table! You – take out the dog!"

"Ma'am! Yes, ma'am!"

That structure is important. For the nuclear family, there must be a chain of command that is, at once, rigid and flexible.

Let's take a hypothetical nuclear family, consisting of a married man and woman and two young school-age children, one male and one female. Let's give them a dog. Let's also give the man or woman an older female relative who periodically comes to visit and stays for a few days.

The thirteenth edition of Combat Leader's Field Guide is a larger format than the earlier pocket size editions Ahern has had for about 40 years. A good resource for protecting the nuclear family.

COMBAT LEADER'S FIELD GUIDE

13TH EDITION

Sgt. Maj. Brett Stoneberger, USA (Ret.)

As we're making a command structure, let's keep in mind the concept of delegation of authority and remember, too, that a command structure that cannot adjust to changes in tactical conditions will have a drastically reduced potential for survival.

Further, let's say that the husband in the nuclear family works some distance away from the home, or even must go out of town on business several days each month. Let's make the wife a stay-at-home mom who has an internet business on the side.

The first thing to do is for the husband and wife to share their questions and concerns regarding their family during a crisis situation. A family is not a democracy, but a marriage should be a partnership. It must be determined who will be in charge of the troops in an emergency, because two people making opposing decisions leads to paralysis, and that costs precious time. In most traditional nuclear families, the husband/father will assume the mantle of leadership (in most cases, too, because his wife lets him). But, remember, the husband works a good distance away from home and is sometimes out of town. The wife, second-in-command in this context, must be completely prepared to assume full command in his absence, whatever the reason may be. This is not a new or unfamiliar role for most modern women.

That basic command structure established, it's time for a family meeting. If the older female relative really does spend several days and nights a year visiting, at least make the effort to include her in the planning, if for no other reason than to let her know what to expect.

In the nuclear family meeting with the kids present, the command structure is explained and authority – read as "responsibility" – is assigned to both children. This can consist of really important tasks with children old enough to assume a good measure of responsibility, or just things that will keep younger and less capable children safely out of the way. Remember, if a child has responsibilities he or she can honestly perceive as important, the child will quite probably rise to the occasion. Our oldest grandchild recently turned 13. He has always risen to the occasion when younger children in his family needed help or attention. He's a responsible person and most children can be, too.

You don't want to frighten your children, so you get input from them, find out what they know and what they might fear in regard to disaster preparedness. Older children who pay attention to news and current events – even slightly – may well have considerable worries regarding disasters. Find out what fears or concerns might exist and make it known that worrying about things is normal. *But the best way to worry less is to take charge of your life and plan for contingencies.* Make working out the procedures your nuclear family will develop and follow in the event of emergency a family activity, something that is serious, but fun – rather than something that is grim.

This is a great time to get out some maps. List frequently visited places – from schools to churches to karate classes to the soccer field or the ballet school or the grocery store – and determine your usual routes to and from these locations. Use a water-based colored felt tip marker to mark your map. Let's

This Coleman tent which is easily erected and has two separate "rooms" can be slung, poles and all, over the shoulder. It is not extraordinarily heavy, but is not something you'd want to carry a long distance by hand. A tent such as this is ideal for bad times and great for family fun and good times.

suppose that primary routes will be in light green. Now, determine alternate routes. Mark the secondary route in orange. If a satisfactory tertiary route presents itself, mark it accordingly in a third color. Don't get carried away. It's not practical to mark out routes to and from the eye doctor you only see once a year. You'll need copies of these maps in each family vehicle and in the house. You can always digitally photograph the maps and run smaller-sized copies that can be read with the aid of a pocket magnifying glass, these smaller maps being easily carried on your person, if needed.

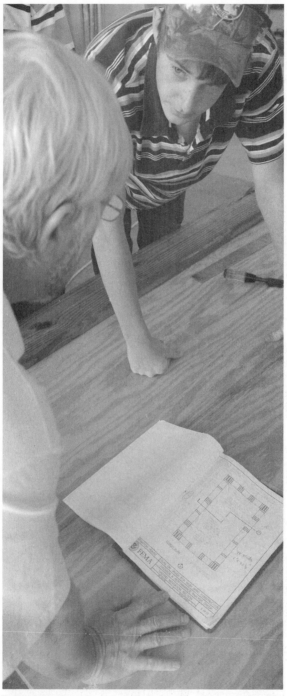

Formulating an emergency plan and going over it with your nuclear family is key to disaster preparedness.

Photo courtesy FEMA News Photo

If this is beginning to seem like a lot of bother, remind yourself that we're talking about the safety of your loved ones. There is nothing on this Earth more important than that.

Using these same maps, determine rendezvous points in the event everyone cannot make it home or making it home would put your nuclear family at greater risk. Establish rendezvous procedures and protocols. Your children should already have code words they'll keep more secret than any computer password. If the possibility exists that a neighbor or friend might have to include your children in their family on an emergency basis, make certain this trusted person has the code words or phrases.

It's time for your first field exercise, one you should repeat periodically so the lesson of the exercise will not be forgotten. Walk or drive to your emergency rendezvous points, starting at places your children might be without you.

You cannot make emergency kits for your children to carry with them to school, but you can make emergency kits for them that can be kept in the family vehicles or at home or both. These kits will be modified to suit the ages of the children in question. Handheld puzzles or games should be included, as well as crayons and paper for younger kids..

Remember the family relative who comes to visit? Make up a kit for her, as well. When she's under your roof, she's your responsibility. If she has prescriptions, encourage her to make certain she has an adequate supply with her when she visits, along with anything else she needs to maintain basic daily health.

Much the same holds true for the family dog. Have some treats that are rotated in and out of the kit on the same schedule as your trail mix bars and water get rotated. Honey the Wonderdog loves Milk Bone Dog Biscuits and they are both portable and nutritious. Include some sort of container into which water can be placed so the dog can drink. In a pinch, a large fast food drink cup can be used to water a dog, but it's not too terribly efficient. If the dog takes any sort of regular medication, use the same sort of rotational plan as you use with your own medications in your kit.

Every family should run emergency drills. If you cannot instantly know what you would do in the event of a house fire, how you would evacuate – how you would keep track of everyone – if you are not prepared? Practice such drills. Chances are that your local fire department can give you some terrific

If you have a dog the size of Honey, a motorized evacuation will require a good sized vehicle. If your dog is older, a protracted evacuation on foot could prove problematic.

ideas. If you have second floor bedrooms, for example, you need a flexible ladder and everyone in the family who is physically capable should practice using it. That older female relative and the family dog? The older female relative would be safer sleeping on the ground floor. A small dog can be carried out. A large dog may have to fend for itself; but, dogs are pretty smart when it comes to getting away from fires.

Make sure that smoke alarms are in working order; most professionals advise you to check batteries frequently and change out batteries roughly every six months. But a fire drill is only one kind of drill. If you're going to prepare, you need practice. Explore what happens if you find yourself trapped in a room and your escape route is compromised. Teach nuclear family members how to safely test a door in order to determine if there's fire on the other side. Your fire department can help you once again with learning such procedures.

Children love games and adults also tend to loosen up if an activity is presented in a fun way. Role playing can be incorporated with these drills and they can be turned into festive family fun. Once a month, why not make dinner outside on the Coleman stove and eat by candle and lamp light? If it's really cold weather, but not dangerously so, get out the serious cold weather gear. Toast each other's health with water from your canteens. Keep all the lights off, simulating a power outage, and listen to your battery-operated or crank-powered radio. This can be a great time to forget the television or the video games for a few hours and re-connect. If the kids fall asleep, it can be a great time for a little romance, too – if the older relative isn't visiting this week.

I'm referring to things like Coleman stoves and canteens and emergency lighting. Every home needs these items. Odd as it may seem, there are people who don't even have a work-

Ahern with Honey the Wonderdog, who is not fat but very big and weighs over 100 pounds. Honey takes up the entire back seat of this mid-size car.

A fire extinguisher in the kitchen is a must and several fire extinguishers should be positioned around your home, in bedrooms and elsewhere.

ing flashlight available to them. Most times, it's not because they can't afford a flashlight or fresh batteries for an existing flashlight. Often, the absence of a functioning flashlight with extra fresh batteries and replacement bulbs is nothing more than carelessness. Every time there's a chance of an evening thunderstorm, hence the possibility of a loss of electrical power, I keep a small flashlight in my pocket or on a table easily within reach.

Have a plan for the everyday necessities. If disaster strikes and the stores are closed or you can't get to them, do you really want to run out of toilet paper three days from now? How about feminine hygiene products? Don't count on borrowing the necessities from your neighbors, because they may be even less well-prepared and might even figure they can borrow from you.

Preparedness can be fun. The absence of preparedness can instantly and very unpleasantly personalize the concept of disaster for your nuclear family. What possible benefit is there to being helpless before man and nature? If you have a family, being unprepared for life's little unpleas-antries is abdicating an important responsibility. Guarding one's family is an instinct we all have as human beings and as parents.

Using a larger fire extinguisher, Ahern aims the hose nozzle.

CHAPTER 5:
EXTENDED FAMILY PREPAREDNESS

In the context of disaster preparedness, what is your extended family? Whom do you include? My wife Sharon and I live in northeast Georgia. Some of our closest and dearest friends live in places as distant as suburban Chicago and suburban Seattle, while other friends, about whom we care deeply live, in Augusta, Georgia, which in the event of a disaster might as well be on the dark side of the moon. Under optimal conditions, Augusta is close to two hours away by automobile. In the event of a disaster, main arteries would be choked. If the power went out for the entire Eastern seaboard, our friends in suburban Chicago and suburban Seattle quite possibly would be unaffected. Our friends in Augusta would be in the same boat we are, except for the fact that Augusta is a good-sized city and cities are far more dangerous places to be in the event of disasters, natural or man-made.

Determining who is in your extended family group is not something to be approached lightly, and it may make for some unpleasant choices. Maybe your great Aunt Sadie or good old Uncle Bob lives on the other side of town and getting to them might be so potentially perilous as to jeopardize your nuclear family. Tough moral choices here.

The continued survival of the nuclear family is of paramount importance. Therefore the composition of the extended family must be weighed carefully. In the previous chapter, which dealt with the nuclear family, the occasional visits from an older female relative were part of the planning. But the type of disaster and how much time, or how little time, there might be to prepare must be taken into account when planning for the extended family's survival.

Let's say that the United States' relations with Russia were to go terribly wrong suddenly and the two nations were poised on the brink, as they were during the Cuban Missile Crisis, when John Kennedy and Nikita Khrushchev held the fate of the world in their hands and a thermonuclear war was staring us in the face. With such a situation of heightening tensions, there would very likely be sufficient warning

During a crisis, extended family members may be forced from their homes and turn to you for guidance. Photo courtesy FEMA News Photo

that the extended family could be gathered in the potentially safest available location. For example, our son and his wife and children live quite a bit closer to a major city – Atlanta – than we do. Our nephew lives even farther away from a major city. Given the time, extended family plans might include our son's nuclear family and our daughter's nuclear family getting together with our nephew at his potentially safer location. Yet the concept of extended family could be quite a bit broader. Should Sharon and I be included in this extended family unit? What about our daughter-in-law's and our son-law's parents? Our daughter-in-law has a brother, our son-in-law has a brother and a sister. All those siblings are married and there are a number of children. Do we all get together and form a tribe?

Where does the extended family stop? Again, determining this can only be done in the light of the nature of the disaster being faced.

After wrestling with these moral and emotional issues, and arriving at less-than-perfect answers, of course, the first step is to establish the extended family chain of command. Using our own nuclear family – Sharon and I and our dog, Honey – as a model, I'll assume our son's nuclear family and our daughter's nuclear family and our nephew's nuclear family combine with ours to form the extended family. Establishing chain of command would be somewhat difficult, since our son and our son-in-law are both quite competent men and display good judgment. The same is true of our nephew. If you are establishing a chain of command, be prepared to accept the fact that the best figure at the top of the chain might not be you. Be open-minded about the strengths and weaknesses of yourself and others.

Whoever is at the top of the extended family chain of command and the rest of the command structure – everybody not too old or too young to be involved unless the extended family is comparatively large – needs to determine several basics. First, all must agree on the composition of the extended family. All may not like it, but all need to agree to accept it. This could be a thorny problem, but the time to address it is when you are not trying to cope with a disaster.

Remember to take into consideration the delegation of authority, which will be more important in this larger, extended family group.

Of paramount importance is the establishment of criteria concerning what will trigger your extended family's emergency response. Remember the story we've all grown up with, about the little boy who cried "wolf." If we have too many false alerts, after a time the alert may be ignored or the response tardy – neither of which is desirable.

Just as with the nuclear family, the extended family needs to establish routes and rendezvous protocols, based on and interwoven with what already exists at the nuclear family level.

Broader emergency drills need to be conducted. These can be done as a vacation experience over a long weekend. Again, if the tone that's set is one of fun and excitement rather than gloom and doom, everyone can have a beneficial experience that will be remembered happily and will prove useful in the event of that real emergency coming along as a challenge to the extended family.

National Preparedness Month
Are you ready?

CHAPTER 6:
COMMUNITY PREPAREDNESS

The nuclear family is a component of the extended family. As circumstances may or may not dictate, the extended family may or may not be able to function as a component of the prepared community. But, almost certainly, the nuclear family will be an element of the prepared community. The prepared community can be as simple an entity as a few city blocks organized for survival and protection or an aggregate of nearby farms or ranches. The prepared community may encompass an entire sub-division – a "neighborhood" in the real estate sense – or a political sub-division, as in a small town or larger civil entity. What works at the neighborhood level can be scaled up for larger communities, or scaled down in order to meet the needs of smaller groups.

If the extended family is, at least somewhat, like a tribe, then the prepared community is even more tribal in its structure. In a tribe, everyone has a role. Some may be hunters and warriors, some may be gatherers, some medicine men or mid-wives, but each has his or her role. For the prepared community to be a fully functional organization for common survival and, if necessary, common defense, following the tribal model – updated, of course, to modern requirements – is a necessity.

The prepared community must first organize itself. To do that, it must be purpose-oriented and, once that purpose is generally agreed upon by the organizers, a chain-of-command established. It must be remembered that many persons are, or may become, distrustful of the concept of a community organizing itself for survival purposes in the event of a natural or manmade disaster. Once the idea of establishing guidelines and procedures in the event common defense becomes necessary or prudent, certain individuals within the community and some persons or bodies within the civil government structure may find themselves to be wary.

Organizers must make certain that the term "prepared community" is not perceived as a euphemism for "militia." There are no politics involved in the prepared community.

I'm very outspoken politically. So are many other people. Still others hide their politics for various reasons, or feel that political discussion is too provocative. In the context of the prepared community – for mutual survival and security to truly be effective – differences must be set aside, political differences being one of these. The only critical political concern – perhaps better

Prepared community members line up for federal disaster assistance.
Photo courtesy FEMA News Photo

described as a social philosophy factor – is that point of view which holds that all survival, protective and security functions are the exclusive prerogative of this governmental entity or that. Many people who believe this avoid the idea of taking individual responsibility for such matters, seeing such planning as being somehow too right-wing and, therefore, too suspect.

In fairness, some people on the right aren't immune to this sort of thinking and equate the word "liberal" with abysmal stupidity. Neither way of thinking is very productive, and in the context of people joining forces temporarily for their common good, such opinions can even be harmful. Even if only temporarily, the old aphorism, "Nothing makes friends like a common enemy" couldn't be truer than in the case of uniting against natural and manmade disaster.

The chain-of-command for the prepared community only comes into play as relates to preparation to survive natural and manmade disasters – nothing more. That must be made clear in order for your prepared community to function, regardless of the individual political and social outlooks of the members of the community.

That said, there are aspects of military organization which can well be assimilated into the organization of the prepared community. For example, all military personnel must learn the fundamentals of basic First Aid procedures. Small military units will have non-physician medics attached, while larger units will incorporate actual medical doctors. Treatment of the injured or wounded might start with one "trooper" performing basic First Aid on another until a medical corpsman can take over. If the injury is sufficiently severe, the injured trooper moves up to the next level of care. This might be a field hospital or an evacuation to a fully staffed permanent facility, both these latter staffed by medical doctors and nurses.

In a time of crisis, whether the disaster is manmade or natural, medical facilities – urgent care, emergency rooms, etc. – will be glutted with patients. The time required for EMTs (emergency medical technicians) to arrive will be extended dramatically, assuming such help can get to your prepared community.

One of the first steps to be undertaken once the prepared community's chain-of-command is established will be the recruitment of personnel with a medical specialty. Ideally, you'll find a retired physician whose wife was a registered nurse. It would also be great to find an oral surgeon, a dentist and a dental assistant, since tooth-related problems often seem to arise at the most inconvenient times in the normal course of events. A veterinarian and a veterinary assistant would be great to have, too. Aside from keeping the prepared community's pets well and healthy, veterinarians can serve as meat inspectors. This could be useful in the event that deer or other game animals or domestic livestock must be incorporated into a possible nutritional plan for the prepared community. Additionally, most veterinarians can do more than a little human doctoring – they likely won't want to, of course – in a pinch.

Whether your prepared community incorporates such skilled persons or not, you'll also want to identify and encourage participation from any retired police, fire, EMT, or military personnel. Active duty police, fire, EMT and military personnel may well be initially absent or subsequently called away during times of emergency.

Say that you are blessed or lucky enough to find four or five persons with the required medical skills. It must then be determined who will logically be best to serve as the medical team leader. In turn, the medical team leader should work with his/her colleagues to determine preventive medicine practices, construct emergency procedures and compile equipment and supply lists.

Other occupational specialties will also prove invaluable. Some of these include carpenters, plumbers, electricians and anyone in the building trades. One of the most basic of human needs is shelter. In the event of terrific storms, that need for shelter will still have to be met. Some of the other specialties which can prove invaluable include, but are not limited to, child care professionals (to watch the little kids while their parents and older children are also busy working on behalf of the prepared community); caterers or cafeteria workers (who can safely prepare and serve mass quantities of healthful food when nuclear family meal-taking becomes impractical for one reason or another); clergy (in times of crisis, spiritual well-being and comforting are always important); automotive mechanics (to keep the rolling stock rolling); computer and information technology specialists (as long as the internet is still up and there is electrical or battery power to access it, news and information about the crisis would be vital); experienced hunters, fishermen and trappers (in an extended crisis, one lasting several weeks or months, wild game could factor in as an extremely important dietary component); and a handyman (the sort of person who can fix practically anything with practically nothing could become the most popular guy around). Another bit of intelligence to develop concerning potential assets in your prepared community is locating sources for discounts on everything from foodstuffs to medical supplies to ammunition.

Depending on the season and the duration of the crisis, the successful backyard gardener could be one of your prepared community's truly important assets. Even in a modern subdivision or neighborhood, in which the typical lot is reasonably small, there's always room for a lawn. Beautiful green lawns look luxurious; they are also useless as people food or pet food. But the ground in which your crabgrass grows is fertile. If it is likely that the impact of the disaster will affect the availability of fresh produce for a significant period, convert some of that wasted ground that always seems to need mowing into nutritious crops you can pick. Be careful about fertilizer and other additive-related safety factors. Bush beans, pole beans, tomatoes, zucchini, squash and a host of other vegetables grow in virtually any temperate climate, given a modest amount of care and the proper seasonal temperatures.

If you can find just some of these people, count your blessings. Even if you can't, you need to parlay those skills that are available within the prepared community so that such basic functions can be filled.

If a security function is necessary, only those persons with a maturity and skill level that can be relied on should undertake to handle it, let alone plan it.

Any security for the prepared community should be kept extremely low-key, unless conditions dictate otherwise. Remember, the idea is to get through the disaster in one piece and get life back to normal as quickly as possible. Sadly, there will always be people who are unprepared, for whatever reason, and who will, when necessary, try to take all or part of what those who prepared have put away. No matter your philosophical or religious beliefs, to ignore that is to do so at your own risk and the peril of your loved ones.

Once your prepared community's structure is in place, it is not only prudent but necessary that the concept of the drill, which we've already discussed, be explored, planned and implemented.

Unlike the nuclear family or even the extended family, the prepared community's drills will be more challenging logistically becauuse of the very number of people involved and their age range.

Make the drills fun. Security drills, for example, can involve water guns (paintball is too messy for houses, sidewalks and lawns). Kids of all ages can always have fun with a water gun. With security drills, any former military personnel – if they can keep a "light" approach – can be of positive value.

Full-tilt drills can be part of what used to be called a "block party," where part of a street is closed off (with appropriate legal permission, of course) and you have food and games for the children and music and all the things you'd have at a party that's family oriented. If the majority of people on your "block" are with you concerning the concept of the prepared community, some of the activities can be related to skills that need practicing. If alcohol of any kind is available, there should be nothing to do with firearms or vehicles or anything else which could result in liability.

Games can include contests to see who can tie the most square knots in 30 seconds, who has the fastest time climbing down an emergency fire ladder, or other fun but purposeful games. Don't belabor preparation for disaster, but take advantage of the opportunities that present themselves for fine-tuning your prepared community.

CHAPTER 7:
EMERGENCY COMMUNICATIONS

Information is vital. Without "intel," you are operating from a losing position at the get-go. In the context of disaster preparedness, however, advance information will not always be available. X-ray emissions within a solar flare erupting from our sun's surface would reach Earth in seconds and a Coronal Mass Ejection (CME), with an average speed of one million miles per hour,

Ahern tunes in the family's vintage SounDesign shortwave and marine band radio. After more than 35 years, it still works and can be used to pick up broadcasts from within the United States and outside the country. You still have to fiddle with the antenna and tuning can be a challenge, but with a new unit to connect to AC household current, this radio has a lot of life left in it.

would reach Earth in but a few days' time. CMEs are giant gas bubbles laced with clouds of magnetically charged particles, their mass measured in billions of pounds, their greatest speed as much as two million miles per hour. According to NASA, a CME can produce an explosive force equivalent to "one billion hydrogen bombs." Other issues – such as health concerns for pilots and astronauts – aside, solar flares or CMEs can seriously disrupt communications and could even knock out satellites and disrupt the power grid and introduce electrical currents into large metal structures. How do you prepare your communications options for something like that?

The potential for CMEs reaches its peak at the peak of an 11-year solar cycle. That peak should be sometime before 2012. Given the totally non-ideal situation, a giant economy-size CME could play havoc with power and communications while compressing the magnetosphere on the northern side of the planet and extending it on the southern side. This would be a temporary manipulation, of course, and would result in "Northern Lights" for the southern hemisphere until the phenomenon fully passed.

An enemy attack utilizing a high altitude thermonuclear blast to create an electro-magnetic pulse would erode and eventually destroy communications within the affected area. There are various concerns about this occurring. One theory is that a small nuclear weapon, accurately launched and detonated at 300 miles up – something quite possible for a rogue nation's missile capabilities, if it has the warhead – would be all that is necessary to knock out technology for quite a bit of the United States. Modern solid-state electronics are vastly more vulnerable than their tube-type predecessors of the pre-solid state days.

When the NOAA weather radio alerts us to a Severe Thunderstorm Warning, we should take appropriate precautions. When the alert is a Tornado Watch, we need to be extremely vigilant. When there is a Tornado Warning, we really do need to take cover. Check with your local fire department or emergency services people and ask about the NOAA Spotters Program. You take a brief course – free – on weather-related phenomena and you get a phone number you can call if you spot something in the sky. You may also be contacted to observe and notify if you see, for example, what may be the formation of a funnel cloud. Your weather radio will tell you if other spotters are being activated or not. A generally accepted axiom in weather forecasting is that the more detailed information that is reported accurately, the greater the probability of a forecast being correct. "Skywarn" is one government program that really makes sense and is of great potential value to the community.

But emergency signals on your weather radio aren't the only source or type of necessary intelligence. The prudent person who is interested in living a long and happy life tries to be aware of his or her surroundings at all times. These days, in many ways, our surroundings are the entire world.

We can get long range weather forecasts – anything much over three days is more speculation than prognostication – that will allow us to be alert for trouble far more in advance than ever before, and with greater potential for

The Radio Shack emergency weather radio.

accuracy. If we know that a front that spawned several tornados is 12 hours away from us, then we know that in less than 12 hours we should be especially vigilant and plan accordingly.

Hypothetically speaking, of course, let's say FOX News broadcasts information concerning a potential meltdown at a nuclear power plant that is an hour's drive away. Or perhaps the local news tells us that there has been an expressway/freeway accident not far from us involving a chemical tanker truck and there is risk of a hazmat (hazardous materials) incident for persons in the surrounding area. Or maybe we learn that a hurricane has just moved inland. Although we're in no danger from the hurricane itself and no Tornado Watch or Tornado Warning has yet been issued, as a precaution, we keep the radio turned to an all-news station when we drive to school to pick up the kids or drive to the grocery store. We are informed because we choose to be and we can be alert for a problem which might negatively impact our lives.

Information is delivered to us in various ways. We can arrange to have emergency weather bulletins or news headlines sent to our cellular telephones. We can have alerts come to us on our computers. We want to keep informed of a developing situation and we can merely pop over to a news website and have some of the latest data available to us instantly.

During the urban unrest of the 1960s, my wife Sharon worked for an organization that had a news wire service telex (an electric keyboard being actuated by a telephone line, if you are too young to remember such technology). Many times, she'd get bulletins coming in over the wire that were designated "not for publication." Maybe the information in these news flashes was not for publication, but it was sometimes handy to know about.

In a crisis that turns into a survival situation, standard means of communication may very well be wholly down or severely compromised. Various natural phenomena can knock out satellites and electrical power. Sabotage can do the same. Telephone land lines run on different circuitry than your household current. It would be a rare occurrence – read that as "extremely serious" – for regular electricity and telephone land lines to go out of service essentially simultaneously. That being the case, it is the wise person who keeps an old telephone around. We do and we're glad we did. Not very long ago, we had a storm which knocked out power to some areas for well over a day. Our conventional modern telephones ceased working, because they require household current to power their base stations. One phone actually died because of a surge as the power went out. We remembered that we had a land line telephone we hadn't used for years. We connected the land line phone to the telephone jack and got a dial tone. We were without power, but we had a phone and could save the cellular phone for a real emergency. Certainly, we could have charged a cellular phone off the cigar lighter in the car, but then we would have been using gasoline. Remember, gas pumps need electricity to work, as do cash registers and credit card machines.

If cell phones had gone out, a handy thing to have would be a two-way radio. Citizens Band – CB – radio will only work over comparatively short distances, but it has the potential to keep you in contact with police and other emergency services. Communication between two base stations – let's say your house and the local police department – could take place over a distance as great as 20 miles, if you each have really long external antennae and you're living outside a city. By really long, I mean that it is generally conceded that 15 feet or more of antenna will be necessary for reliable communication at long distances.

Citizens Band is a radio band – a series of frequencies – for personal communication. Did you have a radio-controlled toy car when you were a kid? Its frequency was part of the Citizens Band. The popular conception of CB radio is 23 channels and, in the 1970s, when CBs were at their height of popularity, CB language crept into the common vernacular. "Keep the rubber side down," for example, means "drive safely and don't flip over." These days, there are

The Midland Base Camp radio can be dynamo-operated by means of this hand crank. The Midland radio's controls are simple to use and even the carrying handle makes for a convenient feature when used with the built in flashlight.

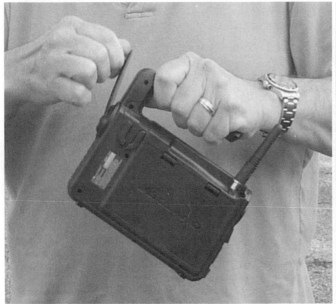

a greater number of frequencies, of course, with specific ones delegated to be used with the ever-widening range of radio-controlled devices. Regular CB has consisted of 40 channels for quite a number of years. But fewer people "have their ears on" in the 21st century because the cellular telephone is so much more versatile – until the cellular system goes down.

The most perennially practical form of private radio is "ham" or "amateur" radio. It is well over a hundred years old and enables the knowledgeable operator to converse with people all over the world, given appropriate atmospheric conditions.

For the person who is paranoid about information censorship – whether justifiably paranoid or not – amateur radio is ideal. Amateur radio is also the backbone of community-based civil defense. Power lines or telephone lines may be knocked down in a storm or sabotaged, but amateur radio can keep on going. If there is no electricity, batteries or low-yield human-powered generators can keep an operator on the air. In a defense emergency, amateur radio must be triangulated in order to actually pinpoint its origin. The equipment can be compact enough that it can be moved by the broadcaster, which makes such location by triangulation extremely difficult.

There is nothing "amateur" about amateur radio, the term deriving from the fact that such radio is not for commercial profit. The then-newly-adopted SOS signal (1908) was not first broadcast in earnest by the iceberg-stricken *HMS Titanic* (1912) as popular mythology would have it. It was broadcast during the *Titanic* disaster, however, alternating with an older distress signal used by the British. Both signals were broadcast in Morse Code as continuous wave (CW) radio telegraphy. CW is used to this day because of the simplicity of its equipment and its international "language" of Morse code. It is interesting to

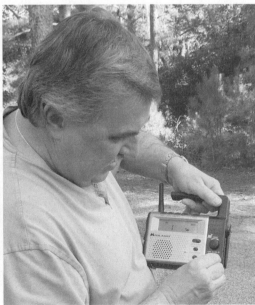

An excellent emergency radio from Eton. Ahern starts to crank the dynamo.

note that amplitude modulation (AM) transmitters – a sort of classic style of transmission – utilize vacuum tubes. In the event of a catastrophic coronal mass ejection or an electromagnetic pulse resulting from a nuclear detonation, assuming there were appropriate vacuum tubes available in a protected drawer somewhere, the amateur radio operator would merely have to remove the spoiled tubes and replace them with fresh ones in order to potentially get back on the air, helping others in the aftermath of tragedy.

There are several approaches to the use of this versatile technology. The "fixed" station can be part of a house, a structure aboard a ship at

The Eton emergency radio with antenna extended and carrying case slung cross body.

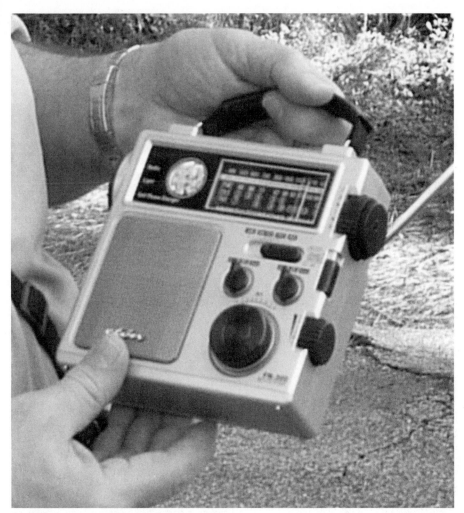

A closer look at the Eton radio's controls.

sea, a "building out back" or anywhere workable. Mobile stations, on the other hand, may be among the most practical as concerns emergency preparedness. Typically, a serious "ham" operator will have a short wave radio in his or her automobile or truck. The actual unit will be in the trunk or under the seat, only the apparatus necessary for two-way communication positioned for easy driver access. Weather spotters are particularly keen on this practice, since this allows virtually instant reporting of dangerous weather phenomena as soon as such phenomena are spotted. Such "mobile" units are commonly set up for voice only.

You need not be a ham operator in order to listen to amateur radio. Sharon and I have a radio that is over 30 years old that we got as a premium with a gasoline credit card. It not only has traditional AM and FM bands, but also short wave bands and marine bands (not the kind of Marine Band that plays

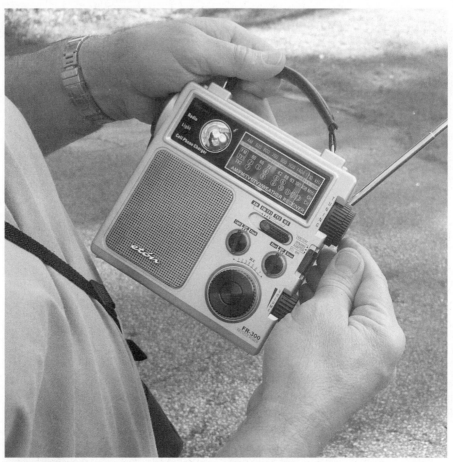

An identification message flashes on the radio from Eton.

Sousa marches). Many is the time Sharon and I have sat around listening to short wave broadcasts from the United States and other parts of the world. It's kind of a neat experience, just listening in – you never know what you'll hear.

Sizes of the actual units range from lower powered, battery operated transmitters not terribly much larger than a cellular telephone to those about the size of two DVD players stacked one upon the other. Convenience is another feature of Amateur radio. There is, of course, the matter of an antenna. When a mobile or hand-held portable unit is in use, there are obvious restrictions on antenna length.

Midland Radio (www.midlandradio.com) offers an interesting product. It features 22 channels compatible with General Mobile Radio Service operation and seven of these are shared with the Family Radio Service. This is a two-way system – it needs to be licensed for use – that will get up to five miles in range, assuming ideal conditions and unobstructed line of sight. Privacy codes can be set on the Midland XT511. Additionally, the XT511 has NOAA All-Haz-

Ahern with the Midland radio plugged in to the cigar lighter to provide emergency weather and FEMA bulletins while on the road.

Ahern listening for a bulletin on the flash flooding that was taking place in Georgia at the time of this photo.

ards/Weather Alert band for automatic reception. Also an AM and FM radio, it doubles as a three-LED flashlight and an alarm clock. There are high and low power settings and the unit can be run on dynamo power alone. Of course there's an AC/DC adaptor, too. An accessory is available for emergency recharging of cellular telephones, via the dynamo. The unit features a convenient handle and a carrying strap and weighs one and one-quarter pounds on the postage scale, without batteries. Approximate dimensions are seven and one-quarter by six and one-half by two inches.

Licensing with the FCC (Federal Communications Commission) for GMRS operation coasts $80 as this is written. The license authorizes the licensee and his or her family – but not employees – to use the GMRS service. There is no proficiency test. Of course, you don't need a license to listen to the WX (NOAA) Weather band or an oldies channel on FM. The XT511 is an extremely versatile unit.

People did, of course, communicate – perhaps not as conveniently – before electronics came along to assist. The telegraph and the landline telephone and international radio telegraphy and other similar ground-breaking discoveries that changed the face of the world have come to be rather "last year" as far as technology goes, just as, in the future, our cellular phones will look as ridiculous as the bag-type portable phones of the 1980s. Some of our current cellular phones look like the communicators used in the original *Star Trek* television series but most look even more modern.

The heliograph – sending signals by bouncing sunlight off a mirror or other shiny surface – was once quite modern, as was the semaphore signal – flags waved in pre-arranged patterns – as were smoke signals. In a situation where all electronic communication that did not initially fail eventually degraded to rarity or non-existence, heliographs and semaphores and smoke might prove very useful. **MTM Molded Products** (www.mtmcase-gard.com) makes a series of MTM Case-Gard Survivor Dry Boxes which are great for storing survival items and also include not only a built-in compass on the lid but a mirror for heliograph signaling on the underside. Heliographic signaling is great for ground to air emergency signaling. But for ordinary communication between individuals or families, the "drop" or "postal drop" could prove useful beyond its original sphere – clandestine lovers and the world of espionage.

Against all school rules, when Sharon and I were seniors in high school, we shared a locker. How risqué! We'd use it as a drop, sometimes, Sharon leaving me a message or just something thoughtful. A drop can be any location to which two or more people are privy, yet the location is not common knowledge.

Communications protocols must be established. If a drop or any other clandestine means of communication is used too frequently, it will cease to be secretive. We'd always look over our shoulders to make sure one of the assistant principals didn't spot us. Drops are often natural and things in nature change. You leave a message under a rock on the hillside. Before the intended recipient can get there to pick up the message and leave a reply, a rain storm comes along and the dirt under the rock and the message with it are lost.

Semaphores, heliographs and the like, in order to be secret, must be encoded. If you don't mind other people "reading your mail," it's not an issue.

Extreme communications methods should be reserved for extraordinary times. However, it is wise to plan ahead. It's only good sense to work out something with the nuclear family or the extended family along the following lines. "In the event I can't make it back from the office to the house and you guys have to evacuate or whatever, try to be at the bridge over the creek on Tuesday morning around seven or eight. If you can't wait that long, leave a message. If you get there and I'm not there yet or haven't left a message...." Think things through. Go to the "bridge over the creek" and search out a good spot to leave messages. A minimal amount of planning for the odd contingency, such as a failure to connect after an emergency or unintended separation even after initially connecting, could prevent the deep trauma of being out of touch with a loved one or friend and the entire gamut of circumstances – possibly tragic – which could result.

CHAPTER 8:
WEBSITES
TO MONITOR

Having the technological means by which to obtain information is, of course, useless without the information itself. It's been said that the key to the acquisition of knowledge is merely knowing the right questions to ask; finding answers is usually comparatively easy.

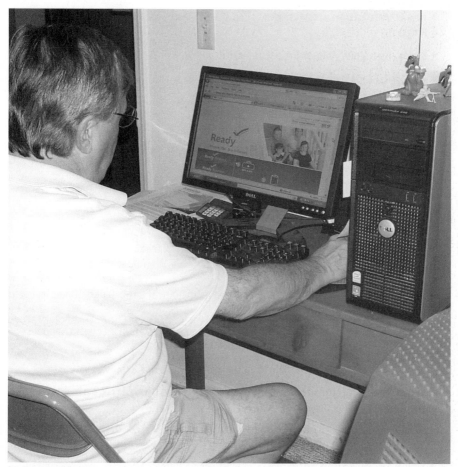

Ahern visiting the www.ready.gov website.

Websites that must be monitored in order to have as much advance warning as possible and for useful information include:

- **www.fema.gov** (Federal Emergency Management Agency)
- **www.weather.gov** (National Oceanic and Atmospheric Administration's National Weather Service)
- **www.nhc.noaa.gov** (National Weather Service National Hurricane Center)
- **www.natice.noaa.gov** (National Ice Center)
- **www.spc.noaa.gov** (National Weather Service Storm Prediction Center)
- **www.intellicast.com** (Intellicast, "the Authority in Expert Weather")
- **www.tsa.gov** (Transportation Security Administration)
- **www.earthquake.usgs.gov** (United States Geological Survey Earthquake Hazards Program)
- **www.volcanoes.usgs.gov** (United States Geological Survey Volcano Hazards Program)
- **www.nps.gov/yell/naturescience** (National Park Service Nature and Science)
- **neo.jpl.nasa.gov/ca/** (NASA Close Objects website)
- **neo.jpl.nasa.gov/orbits** (NASA Near Earth Project Objects website)
- **www.gulfstreamshutdown.com** (Abrupt Climate Change Directory)
- **gcmd.nasa.gov/records/GCMD_MOC.html** (Goddard Space Flight Center Global Change Directory)
- **www.interpol.int/public/Terrorism/default.asp** (INTERPOL Public Terrorism website)
- **www.foxnews.com** (FOX News)
- **news.sky.com/skynews/** (British world news website)
- **www.jerusalempost.com** (Jerusalem Post)
- **www.globalincidentmap.com/home.php** (global terrorism event map; must register)
- **www.nctc.gov/site/index.html\www.terroristwarning.com** (National Counterterrorism Center website)
- **www.travel.state.gov** (US State Department travel advisories)
- **www.washingtonpost.com/wp-dyn/world/issues/terrordata** (Washington Post terrorist attack database)
- **www.mosnews.com** (English language website of Moscow News; a bit flaky but occasionally useful)
- **www.russiatoday.com** (news from a Russian perspective)

Some of these, admittedly, are out-of-the-ordinary websites. There are a lot of choices to be made, too. For news, one might, depending on one's political bent, choose CNN over FOX; I wouldn't. The important thing is to have news from differing perspectives, hence SKY News for the outlook of our most constant ally, Great Britain, and the website jerusalempost.com for things from an Israeli perspective.

As anyone in the intel field will tell you – assuming they are allowed to – intelligence gathering is often the collection of bits and snatches of information that can be assembled into a mosaic of truth. That truth may not be pretty, may, indeed, not be what you wished to find out about in the first place but it is the truth. Should you sit at your computer drowning your sorrows because Yellowstone's earthquake numbers are way up or some of the counter-terrorist websites show data that suggests that a strike is imminent or a news site tells you that NASA is being mum about a Near Earth Object just discovered by an amateur astronomer in Australia? Of course not! Crying in your beer – I'm more of a wine guy, myself – achieves nothing. But, knowing there's something unpleasant afoot or in the offing could mean you'll have a little extra time for your nuclear family or your extended family to finalize preparations, just in case something bad goes down.

What I've done is to put the list included in this chapter into my "Favorites" and look at this one today, that one tomorrow. Some of these are websites I've discovered on my own and some are websites a great old friend with an extraordinarily interesting career background has suggested I might find informative.

If you really want to be well informed, you cannot count on one source to give you all the data you need, no matter how sincerely that source might endeavor to do so. Some of the so-called "mainstream media," both electronic and print, have demonstrated that they will not give coverage to a particular story because it does not coincide with their corporate political views. That's their privilege, of course, but that doesn't help you or anyone else who wishes to be informed for the purposes of staying alive and getting through a crisis. Choose your primary news sources carefully and go to original sources, as much as possible, to supplement and validate what your primary source tells you.

Sometimes it is hard to track down the facts behind a story. The process is called being an intelligent citizen, one who refuses to believe something just because this official or that media outlet says it is so. In a truly dire situation, one with life-changing potential, you must ask yourself if the facts would be released to the public – or would they be "not for publication?"

There's a wonderful old movie, made in 1951, titled *When Worlds Collide*, based on a 1934 novel. The book was a favorite of my dad, Jack Ahern. He thought the movie was okay, too. In it, a scientist discovers that two runaway planets (?) have entered our solar system and Earth will be destroyed. But there is a chance for "rocket ships" to hop to the second of the two planets, where, perhaps, humankind can take root once again. Toward the end of the story, after a lottery has determined who will be allowed aboard the ship and who will be left behind to die, a mob storms the United States' space ship and nearly destroys the last chance for humanity to survive. I believe a lot of world governments would think about that scenario and withhold information that might start a panic. What good would it do for everyone on the planet to know they were in terrible peril? Well, maybe it would do some good. Being informed is our right and our duty as free men and women. Think about it.

Thanks to the internet, cellular technology and other advances, it is becoming harder and harder for news to be "managed," whether by a particular media outlet or a political entity. As long as a free people have broad access to information from around the country and around the world, putting a particular spin on the news and current events is quite a bit more difficult. Certain electronic media outlets actually seem to hide stories from their viewers. If all you rely on for news and current events is a source that doesn't trust you with certain stories or with all the facts, you're crippling your ability to stay informed and be prepared.

Being prepared is the watchword of the FEMA (Federal Emergency Management Agency) READY campaign. The campaign began in 2003 as a joint effort between the Federal Government and the Advertising Council. READY and the Spanish language version, LISTO, promote the idea that people living in the United States should take steps on all levels in order to prepare to withstand emergency situations brought about by natural and man-made disasters. The biggest problem America has as concerns preparedness for such contingencies is that huge numbers of Americans are essentially complacent and don't take any interest in preparedness. A FEMA fact sheet reveals the alarming statistics deriving from an Ad Council survey launched in August, 2008. The Ad Council "...asked Americans in an open-ended question why people are not doing more to prepare. Half of respondents (52%) said that it is because people believe that they are unlikely to be affected by an emergency. Another 21% said that people were too busy (11%) or apathetic (10%)." The FEMA information goes on encouragingly, indicating that the

percentage of Americans who are taking things seriously and trying to prepare is rising on all fronts.

Homeland Security has developed specific information packages for pet owners, for older Americans and, as indicated elsewhere in this book, although a great deal still has to be done for handicapped persons as well.

READY business is overseen by Homeland Security and works in partnership with business organizations. The intent is to prepare businesses for dangerous contingencies. How many businesses don't have any plan in the event of a tornado warning or a bomb threat? Since more than 99 percent of all the employers in the United States are classifiable as small businesses and account for approximately 75 percent of new jobs added to the economy, according to FEMA and the Small Business Administration (SBA), one can easily see the economic disaster which could be wrought if America's small businesses could not cope with issues raised by natural and man-made disasters. The most im-

Many government and private websites were the first, best source of information on the September 11, 2001, terrorist attacks. Photo courtesy FEMA News Photo

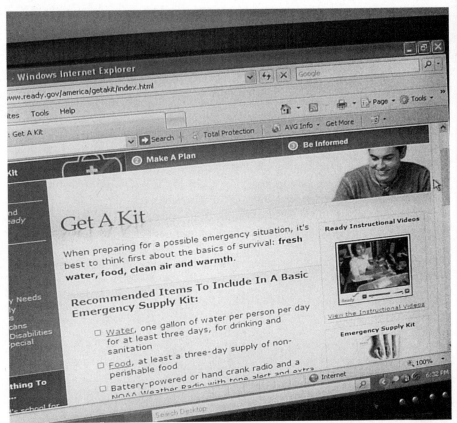

The Ready.gov website tells you to get a kit ready. This time, believe the government!

portant threats addressing business, according to data included in the FEMA website, are fires and cyber attacks. Fifty-five percent of small businesses surveyed indicated that they had taken steps aimed at upgrading their ability to cope with disasters during the year previous to the survey. This is encouraging.

READY KIDS has programs for children grades K through 8 and works with the Sesame Workshop to reach pre-school children and their families. Homeland Security has worked with Scholastic on the development of relevant in-school materials for fourth, fifth and sixth grade students. Two hundred sixty-one thousand middle school teachers have received these materials to incorporate into their curricula.

If you go to the internet and search for survival and disaster preparedness information, you'll find more than you bargained for, much of it very useful. As the old saying goes, however, you must "separate the wheat from the chaff."

Whether it's READY BUSINESS, READY KIDS, or any of the other READY campaign aspects, this is a seriously worthwhile Federal program and should be studied as a significant – but not an all-inclusive – part of your information gathering, so you can be ready!

CHAPTER 9:
FOOD AND WATER

Meals Ready to Eat (MREs) were being sold to Americans who wanted to be prepared.

Essential to survival under any circumstance, ordinary or dire, are food and water.

Determining the amount of food and other essentials is discussed elsewhere in this book. But what are you actually going to put away that won't necessarily require refrigeration?

For an anticipated short duration situation, you may want to consider specially prepared meals. **Mountain House** is a name that instantly comes to mind. During the run-up to Y2K, Mountain House products (www.mountainhouse.com) were in historically great demand. As the world draws closer and closer to December 21, 2012 (the end date of the Mayan Long Count Calendar, considered by some to be an apocalyptic event), the Mountain House people

will likely see epic demand levels once again. If you wish to include Mountain House foods and similar specialty food products – such as MREs – in your preparation for possible natural or manmade disasters, you will very likely want to acquire these products sooner rather than later, not only for better selection, but for basic availability.

The two most popular options are freeze drying and dehydration. (Mountain House Foods are freeze dried.) As more and more people may become interested in putting food away for disaster preparedness, we must also consider the potential for a wide range of other factors to precipitate food shortages. Think of it like an entire continent running to the store and buying up all the bread and milk, but *you* still need bread and milk because you haven't gotten around to getting yours yet.

Mountain House has been around for more than three decades. Some of the food that they produced decades ago is still in storage and, although

Three Mountain House selections with a Mountain Oven, which requires no heat source.

Mountain House doesn't particularly push the idea of holding onto their food for decades, we learned that some of the food Mountain House made during the Viet Nam War had been tried and essentially tasted as good as it should and was just as healthy. Of course, shelf life of such an amazing time also depends on the specific type of Mountain House food and the conditions under which it was stored.

Another source for freeze dried food that is well respected is **Alpine Aire** (www.alpineaire.com). **Rainy Day Foods** (www.waltonfeed.com) specializes in dehydrated food, packed in bulk. The dehydration process is less expensive than the individual meal approach taken with freeze drying. Freeze drying is quite an ancient practice, yet as modern as superconductors because freeze dried food weighs less than food that is normally hydrated.

The freeze drying process can occur naturally or be induced artificially. Not only can food be freeze dried, but blood plasma and other medical related items can benefit from the process as well. When the process occurs naturally, the food freezes in cold temperatures and the water within it turns to vapor. The people who make freeze dried foods for the astronauts and for the rest of us use specially designed machines which incorporate the means for freezing the food and some type of vacuum pump for extracting all the moisture. Today, there is everything from freeze dried ice cream to freeze dried coffee.

The key to making freeze dried foods work is effectively sealing them against moisture. You can have freeze dried meats and fruits and anything that you might normally eat that would require refrigeration, yet you need no refrigeration. The weight consideration is very serious if you find yourself in a situation where you must evacuate and every ounce is important.

Dehydration, on the other hand, is far less costly. It is unlikely that anyone reading this will run out to freeze dry their own food, but Sharon and I, like a great many people, have a food dehydrator and have successfully dehydrated both meat

This Alpine Air dish comes in its own cooking pouch.

An Equi-Flow food dehydrator can be used to make anything from jerky to candy-like fruit snacks. Whatever you make with this can be used in a variety of ways as trail food, or for adding to venison or other game in order to vary the taste.

and fruit with very little difficulty. Although you can build your own dehydrator, the commercial kind will be most people's best choice. If you live in a climate where it gets really hot, and you don't mind stinking up your vehicle, you can dehydrate food in an emergency under the windshield of your sealed tight automobile. This idea does not appeal to me personally, but it's useful to know you can do it.

Another technique for dehydrating without a dehydrator is to put the strips of fruit or meat outside on a piece of aluminum foil and cover them with cheesecloth. Plug in an electric

With the front of the unit open, you can see the dehydration trays and, at the rear of the unit, the fan.

(above) Ahern isn't ready to roll the dice – he's mixing potable water with an included salt tablet so he'll be ready to use the Mountain House Mountain Oven.

(left) Ahern pulls out one of the Mountain Oven activation pads before putting it into the Mountain pouch.

fan to blow across the food and this will help to keep flies away. This is the air current technique for repelling insects used in traditional primitive jerky production. The jerky would be positioned where a breeze would blow across it to achieve approximately the same effect as the fan.

Dehydration has advantages that go beyond disaster preparedness. Dehydrated small pieces of watermelon and bananas and similar fruits make a wonderful, tasty and healthy candy substitute for kids. With this basic type of dehydration, you will probably not bother rehydrating. The process of putting the food in your mouth and chewing it will restore a perfectly adequate amount of moisture to jerked meat or dehydrated fruit.

The one problem with some dehydrators is that they are a little noisy because they incorporate a small fan that blows across the items to be dehydrated. The other problem is you will be constantly smelling what is being dehydrated if you are nearby.

More so with freeze drying than dehydration, when you rehydrate, you will restore more of the food's original smell.

Mountain House Foods are not plain foods, but such things as beef stroganoff and chicken teriyaki are staples of the line. Mountain House prepares its entrees in its own cooking facility and now recommends a seven-year shelf life for their pouched foods. Food that they've packaged in their air tight cans, however, can last a lot longer. Mountain House stands by a 25-year shelf life for these canned products and their own testing done by an independent university reveals that actual 30-year-old product stored, as Mountain House puts it, "…under real-world conditions," was still perfectly fine.

Mountain House gives you all the nutritional information for their wide range of products. For example, chicken polynesian, with a net weight of 4.66 ounces, with a half-pouch serving size, has 270 calories. The chart gives you all the information on saturated fat, cholesterol, sodium, fiber, you name it. If you were to eat nothing but Mountain House foods, you'd probably be healthier than you are already. For persons concerned about allergies or who may have a religious objection to shellfish, for example, Mountain House provides a full list of allergen information for all their foods.

Mountain House works closely with READY AMERICA. The Department of Homeland Security and the Advertising Council have created instructional videos that are designed to help people to respond to any emergency. Mountain House also has a special 72-hour emergency meal kit, which contains breakfast and vegetables and lunch and dinner entrees. They also produce the Mountain Oven. The Mountain Oven is flameless and works with Mountain House Foods in the flat-bottom stand-up pouch. There is no need to heat water and the Mountain Oven can be used up to five times. To use it, just add regular drinking water from your canteen or other reliable source. Then, using the heat activation pad, water and a dissolved salt tablet, pour the salted water onto the heat activation pad, close it up tightly and, in 20 minutes, you have a hot meal without a stove or any flame.

(left) Ahern pours the water and salt tablet mixture into the Mountain Oven.

(below) Ahern closes the Mountain Oven packet.

The first time we ever used Mountain House foods was 30 years ago. Caught in an ice storm unexpectedly, we almost went over a bridge. Getting our battered car off the median strip, we were able to pull off the interstate to what was not the world's best motel. As we were preparing to enter our room, two guys actually tried to mug us. Sharon and I actively discouraged them from pressing on with their intentions. By that time, unable because of the ice to even cross the parking lot to get to what passed as a restaurant, the whole family sat down to a gourmet meal in the motel room. The Mountain House food we'd packed along was worth its weight in gold.

But, you don't need to buy specialty foods with a super-long shelf life or dehydrate your own foods. In the run-up to Y2K, it was not uncommon to see people picking up an entire flat of canned vegetables that

Look closely above the Mountain Oven packet and you will see steam rising from two vents in the packet, as the kit does its work.

Ahern removing the lasagna from the Mountain Oven.

were on sale or see giant economy deals on Ramen noodles. What you want is something that is nutritious, tastes good and is inexpensive enough that you can buy a lot of it. When planning for nutrition during a short to medium duration disaster scenario, it's perfectly fine to buy cans of anything from sardines to tuna to Spaghetti-Os. The important considerations are 1) that people will eat it; 2) it has nutritional value; and 3) you can rotate it through your family in the normal course of events. You should watch that cans do not develop swelling, discoloration or rust and give yourself a definite shelf life limit. Logic would suggest that you would be well on the safe side in planning to rotate every three months.

Shelf life for canned goods depends on the contents of the can. First of all, you want to keep any food that you're saving – whether it's specialty survival foods such as those mentioned earlier in this chapter or the on-sale stuff you pick up in the grocery store – in a cool, dark storage area. Generally speaking, the more acidic the food, the shorter its shelf life. Many sources recommend that acidic foods in jars and non-acidic food in cans will remain perfectly edible for at least 24 months, if stored under proper conditions. Even if the food is beyond 24 months old but it looks okay, doesn't smell bad and hasn't discolored the container, it is probably fine to fill up your stomach with.

Over a protracted period of time, foods will leach vitamins and nutrients. But hey! When was the last time you seriously considered vitamins and nutrients when you were looking for a late night snack or a fast food lunch? Occasionally eating some vitamin-depleted foods, just to keep the front and back of your stomach from rubbing together, is not going to hurt you. In general, however, you won't want to push shelf life to the limit or beyond because, in a survival situation, the stamina derived from good nutrition and the boon to overall good health will prove more important than under normal conditions.

As with any food that may be questionable, if you have any reason to suspect it and can safely tell yourself, "I don't need it," dump it. If, on the other hand, food supply is critical and there is no obvious sign that this food will be bad, try only a spoonful or two for taste and to see whether you are suffering no ill effects, after a reasonable period of time. Makes you feel sorry for the First People, doesn't it, when our forebears would send out the guy who wasn't perhaps the brightest ember in the campfire and tell him, "Try those berries over there and see if you get real sick, okay?"

Watch for sales on bulk purchases, but be careful that what you're purchasing hasn't gone through most of its shelf life. Try to buy from major outlets that go through a lot of food quickly.

Be extremely careful when it comes to any product packaged in a sack made of paper or cloth or a cardboard box. Such products are fine in the normal scheme of things, of course, but these containers do not lend themselves to long-term storage. So, for example, if you are going to put away flour, make certain that, once the flour has been acquired, the package is opened and the contents carefully inspected as they are transferred to a clean, dry container that can be sealed airtight. Don't anticipate keeping items like flour, pasta, and sugar or similar items anywhere near as long as you will be able to keep non-acidic canned goods and hermetically sealed foods in jars.

Trying to store water for a protracted period of time is certainly easier, but not without certain limitations. The kind of water that you can buy in little plastic bottles at the grocery stores may or may not be as good as or better than what comes out of your tap. It certainly costs more. I would recommend a couple of alternatives. Certainly, keep your little plastic bottles of water for your daily use. We do, but we also have canteens and large water containers. Elsewhere in this book, I mention carrying an emergency water supply in the vehicle, but we also have an even larger container at the house and we have a number of plastic GI canteens. When Y2K was approaching, we assiduously collected re-sealable bottles which we carefully rinsed, capped and stored over a period of close to a year. Each bottle held three liters of water. By the time Y2K came and went, we had hundreds of liters of water in storage. Had the water supply been interrupted, this water would have been perfectly fine to run through the Katadyn filter or boil and convert to acceptable drinking water or use for such purposes as bathing and what have you.

All this talk of food and water storage is just good common sense under any circumstance. The food that you have put away could be a blessing if your family suffers a temporary economic downturn. A neighboring town, not long ago, had a problem with the water supply. It was drinkable, but its taste was so im-

Whether you've got a lot of space or a little space, whether you plant in the ground or container garden, it's great to have freshly grown vegetables you can trust, season permitting.

possibly bad that restaurants could not offer any beverage that was made with local water. In a situation such as that, having a lot of water put away and the means by which to purify it would sure beat having a cup of coffee or a glass of iced tea that tasted like dirt!

One other long-term food storage technique exists, one that is very little practiced because people are afraid of it. In 2000, the first irradiated meat went on sale to the general public. The process has been around for more than 50 years. Typically, the meat or other food is bombarded with gamma radiation, which kills anything harmful in the food and can enable extremely long storage. I read about a piece of meat that this process was tested on decades ago. It would still be perfectly fine to eat today. It is stored on a shelf at a laboratory and dusted every once in a while. Any bacterium present in irradiated food is killed and anything unpleasant is sterilized. Irradiating food is, quite possibly, the perfect solution to long-term storage problems. Whether or not it becomes acceptable to the general population is another question entirely.

CHAPTER 10:
FOOD PREPARATION

The subject of food preparation should be viewed both in terms of technique and from the standpoint of hygiene.

If you have electricity – which you shouldn't just assume will continue to be available even if it wasn't affected at the outset of an emergency – much of your concerns regarding food preparation will be unaffected. The natural gas supply, although dependent on the industrial computers that distribute it, might or might not be affected during a natural or manmade disaster. You should make certain, however, to have some alternate means of food preparation available to you.

We have four. If our electricity is functioning, Sharon – you don't want to eat my cooking; certainly I don't! – can use our electric stove and we're in business. She can augment that stove with the microwave oven. We also have an old Nesco cooker – a portable electric oven big enough for a turkey – and a toaster oven. The cooker belonged to my mother and we've never used it. The toaster oven, once a hot fad, hasn't seen service in quite a while.

But, let's say that the electricity is taken out of the equation. If that happens, are we stuck with cold food? Certainly not! We have these other ways to prepare hot meals, this discounting the Mountain House Mountain Ovens and the fact that I can go behind our house and gather up wood to build a campfire or a pit and keep either going for quite some time.

Our three other methods of cooking without electricity include a **two-burner Coleman stove,** a **small Weber kettle grill** that burns charcoal briquettes but could use other materials as necessary, and a relatively **large Weber propane grill** that runs off a propane twenty-pounder.

The Weber backyard grill is capable of making anything that you can cook indoors and is fueled by a 20-pound propane cylinder.

A simple means by which to make a meal for two is this charcoal grill from Weber – which is quite small and quite handy.

We keep a spare twenty-pounder on hand and I am planning on picking up yet another one, just in case we need it. For the little Weber kettle, we keep a supply of the kind of charcoal you don't have to use charcoal lighter with. Store that carefully. But, we also keep charcoal lighter fluid – just in case. We have enough of the small Coleman propane cylinders to keep cooking for a very long time and still have a sufficient supply to keep our Coleman lantern running, too.

Okay. So, we've got the equipment to keep cooking. No one functions too well, however, if they themselves are not feeling too well. To prevent that from happening, cleanliness must be of uncompromising importance. If you normally scrape the still-hot grill surface to keep it free of residual food, do an even better job of it in a disaster situation. If you normally let the grill get so hot before you cook on it that no micro-organism could possibly survive, a disaster situation is not the time to skimp on the propane and lower your health safety standards.

If water is in short supply and cleaning pots and pans might be difficult,

A wood stove can be handy for heating or cooking and, when it is not the season to use it, is a perfect place for a grow light and plants. The grow light can be used to start things like tomato plants from seed.

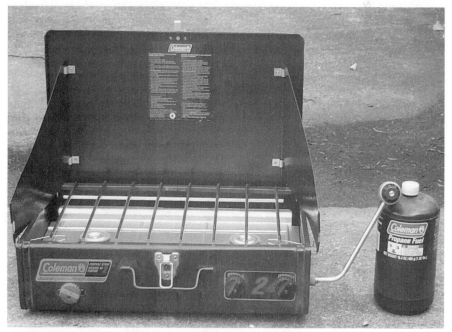

A two-burner Coleman stove with a small propane cylinder.

take your vegetables and wrap them up in **aluminum foil** before putting them on your heat source. Meat can also be cooked in this manner and both the meat and vegetables can go in the same piece of aluminum foil. Putting away a half-dozen or so rolls of aluminum foil isn't wasteful because it's useable in so many ways. You can wrap food in aluminum foil and place it on the coals of an open flame campfire and it will cook and no utensils will have been dirtied. Another advantage of this aluminum foil cooking is that there is no need to apply vegetable-based oil, like PAM, to the grilling surface before cooking. So, you're saving money and having to inventory less product. A win-win situation!

If you can have multiple items cooking or heating at the same time, you're saving fuel resources and aggravation. So you can be cooking meat and vegetables in aluminum foil on the grill while at the same time you were heating up soup in a pan (with no wood or plastic on the handle) and you remembered to pick up everything with extremely heat-resistant equipment. Think and improvise!

This is not a book about wild game preparation, but you might well need to supplement your nuclear family's food supply with fresh meat that can be taken with improvised traps or hunted. We all know the technique involved with making or using an already existing small but sturdy and adequately heavy box, inverting it and standing it up on one edge, the other edge propped up by a stick. A string is tied to the stick and led off some distance from the box. Desirable rabbit bait is placed beneath the box and you wait and wait until the rabbit comes along and goes under the box for the bait. Pull the cord fast and the stick dislodges and the rabbit is trapped under the box. Using a heavy glove, get the rabbit in hand as you raise the box ever so slightly.

Rabbit really does taste like chicken!

Whether you hunt or trap, you must skin and clean the game. Let the animal bleed out, making certain not to open the stomach or intestines, which will contaminate the meat. Watch out for the scent glands. Your knife and your hands should be thoroughly

Two excellent books dealing with wild game.

scrubbed after you remove all the internal organs, without puncturing them. If the water is available to wash out the inside, use it. Grass or safe leaves will work to clean the insides in a pinch. Wipe the cavity dry. Let the animal's body cool down. Ice it, if you can. Make certain that the head is higher than the body, to complete the drainage. You can remove a deer's tongue and clean it merely by washing (no soap, of course) and drying it as needed, then pan-frying or slow-cooking it to have a tasty and nutritious meal right then and there.

If you fish, you must prepare your catch as well, and, depending on the type of fish, carefully filet it. With larger game animals such as deer you'll want to do a full and careful butchering job, circumstances permitting, in a permanent or semi-permanent location, to include removing all the edible meat and organs, cutting up parts for various purposes, packaging everything separately and labeling and storing it at appropriate temperatures. If you are in a hurry and must move on, cut off a haunch and go, however wasteful that may sound. Be careful not to cut at the upper joint, in order to avoid contamination. Cut halfway down what would be analogous to the thigh. You can skin and clean and field butcher later. The haunch can be removed with a sharp, stout knife, or, better still, with your axe.

In a real hurry? Just cut down along both sides of the deer's spine and remove the backstrap – some of the best meat, anyway – and you are on your way. For more detailed butchering of large wild game or domestic cattle, you'll want some good chef's knives of large and medium sizes and a bone saw. To keep the knives sharp and useful, you'll want a good sharpening steel.

Such do-it-yourself meat processing might seem distasteful at first, but after you've had your first foil-broiled venison backstrap or quail shishkebab, you'll agree that it's a skill well worth learning!

CHAPTER 11:
HOW MUCH SHOULD YOU PUT AWAY?

When Y2K was on the horizon, not a few people thought that life would be forever altered, our technology crashing down around our ears and our lives forced to be lived as they would have been in the closing decades of the nineteenth century. Thankfully that did not happen. As this is written, there is widespread concern about the Mayan Calendar's coming to a screeching halt on December 21, 2012. Add to that, the computer model showing the I Ching, an ancient Chinese prediction system, runs out on exactly the same day. If you are reading this after that date, the mathematically obsessive Mayans and the computer model based on the I Ching were, somehow, coincidentally in error or just misunderstood – we hope!

But, barring the end of all time or the total destruction of all life on this planet, or scenarios altering the course of human events for years to come at least, most disasters are comparatively short lived. We cannot put away enough food and other necessary items to sustain ourselves throughout years and years of societal collapse. We might, for example, elect to follow the food storage guidelines of the Mormon church (LDS), in which one analyzes the quantity of food and other basic necessities – everything from rice to pasta to bleach to toilet paper – used per person in order to stockpile a year's supply for an entire family. If this seems a little much, the other extreme is the family that has to run out for supplies every day because buying ahead is impossible due to monetary constraints or because planning ahead was dismissed as paranoid.

As this is written, there are no food shortages in American stores and markets. That could change in a day. Living in the southeast, as we do, the threat of an ice storm is of such concern that, it seems, at the slightest mention of a comparatively minuscule amount of snow in the weather forecast, the population runs out to the grocery stores and purchases bread and milk to the point

Many of the normal things you would keep about the house would be great to put up for emergency use, but packaging determines how long an item can be kept.

that virtually nothing remains on the shelves. We've all seen news footage of areas where hurricanes were expected and people were buying up everything from flashlight batteries to plywood for boarding windows. The point is, if you wait – assuming you have the financial means to do otherwise – you will be inadequately supplied at best, perhaps even finding yourself without the barest necessities for survival.

Assuming you can, how do you go about preparing? Are there formulae? It would seem that whoever in your nuclear family – and this should best be done at the nuclear family level – is most knowledgeable about the nuclear family's nutrition should be the person in charge of this project. Remember, the function of command is the delegation of authority.

The reasoning behind the family nutritionist heading up the operation, in part, is that whoever manages the nuclear family's day-to-day nutrition needs will also know what nuclear family members best enjoy and physically tolerate.

Fish, for example, is universally accepted as a healthy source of protein and other good things for the human body. In my personal case, with the exception of tuna salad, shellfish and – to a lesser degree – salmon, I'm not terribly fond of seafood. Having to live on a diet of which a major component was dried fish would be torture for me. I love grapefruit, but after my heart attack in 2003 – no heart damage and I'm healthier than ever, not to mention no longer smoking – I cannot eat grapefruit because it interacts badly with one of the pills I take each day. Whoever is responsible for determining the nuclear family's nutritional needs will know and consider all these factors.

Next, it must be determined how food will be stored. The storage system must be based on the amount

Some ready-to-go items and the manually operated can opener needed to get into much of what you will put away. Even the Velveeta & Shells is good so long as you can come up with hot water, because it requires no milk.

of storage time before use or rotation, the amount of food needed to be put away in order to sustain the nuclear family for a given period of time, and the climatic conditions under which the food will be stored. The actual containers in which food will be stored and the storage environment all must be taken into consideration.

If you are storing grain or grain-related products, you must realize that vermin go for such items in a big way. Even the best grain-related products that have never been opened can be found to be contaminated in one manner or another, given time – and sometimes not that much time. When Y2K loomed, we bought several boxes of a well-respected brand name pasta product. Six or seven months later, we had to throw away the boxes and their contents. Although never opened, insects were found to be breeding inside one or more of the boxes. As one of my granddaughters would probably put it, *"Ohh, yuck!"* Yuck indeed. Whether little microscopic beasties entered the boxes or were packaged with the product at the factory, the result was the same.

As much as possible, stick to canned goods and foods specifically prepared for long-term storage, in order to be on the safe side as relates to spoilage. If you elect to put away "a year's supply," that's great, but focus on foods regularly consumed within a period of two weeks or a month. Constant rotation has always struck me as the only practical way to approach having large quantities of food on hand for emergencies. Replace what you consume and make certain to consume the oldest items first.

The nuclear family's food needs must be viewed in two possible scenarios. First, the nuclear family will be able to stay in their home for the duration of the disaster event, venturing out as needed, but be able to safely return to home base where food will be stored and prepared.

The second is a much dicier situation. Let's say the disaster requires evacuation to another location or quite a bit of regular movement. What do you do then? Can you lug along with you a few hundred pounds extra worth of food, in addition to water – a gallon weighs 8-1/3 US pounds – and medical supplies and other necessities? We're not even including weapons and ammunition (one round of 5.56mm ball weighs 11.79 grams), assuming these are part of your disaster plan.

Clearly, the prepared nuclear family and extended family may need to consider two separate emergency food supplies. One of these would be for short-term use during an evacuation, the other for longer term use when evacuation would not be necessary. This is neither as difficult nor as expensive as one might suppose. That short-term food supply for the evacuation contingency will be relatively modest, and can be part of the non-evacuation food supply.

If you evacuate on foot, there's a serious limit to the burdens you can handle over several days worth of hiking. I've read accounts of people starting out hiking the Appalachian Trail and, as they went along, finding perfectly good equipment that had been cast aside by earlier passersby because of weight. I knew an Army master sergeant back when I was in high school who told a group of us how he had lightened his load in Korea. He'd been issued an M1 Garand. He swapped it for the smaller and lighter M1 Carbine. He was issued binoculars. He threw away the case. A few ounces here, a pound or two there and it was easier for him to do what he had to do. I don't think I would have made those same choices, but they were his choices to make and not mine.

If you evacuate by automobile, it is entirely likely that at least some of your longer term emergency food supply can come with you. Make certain to have appropriate containers and determine in advance how these containers can be packed in the vehicle while still leaving room enough for the nuclear family – to include the family dog, of course.

Assuming you don't need to evacuate and can take advantage of all your emergency foodstuffs, there are certain precautions that must be observed. Once the power goes out – which it very likely will – as mentioned elsewhere in this volume, you'll have a few hours or so with your refrigerator until you have to start throwing food away as contaminated. There are a few rules to keep in mind.

If you have the means to save refrigerated foods by getting emergency power up and running or adding great amounts of ice to the refrigerator or freezer in order to buy a very little more time at best, do what you can. If that means moving the food to a location where it can be refrigerated, and this can be done efficiently and safely, do it with all speed. Failing all of that, eat what you can while within that first few hours when the food is still good and otherwise keep the door to the refrigerator shut. If the temperature in the refrigerator rises to 40° Fahrenheit or above, the food can make you sick or worse. Dump meat, milk, soft cheese, ice cream, mayonnaise and virtually any dairy product except butter. Shocking as it might be, that includes the pizza left over from yesterday.

Raw vegetables and bread that you might have had in the refrigerator should be consumed as soon as practical. The same holds true for your freezer, only there's a little more time to spare. A half-filled freezer, according to the United States Department of Agriculture guidelines, will be good for 24 hours, with the lid or door closed. A filled freezer will be good for as long as 48 hours. After that, you must discard the food, no matter how wasteful that seems. Frozen food is only safe at 0° Fahrenheit or below.

If you have coolers available – used for anything from tailgate parties during football season to hauling home deer meat – get plenty of ice, if you have advance notice. With ice, you can store meat longer than it will keep in a refrigerator. The coolers will really help. In the event that your power outage has to do with an ice storm or other cold weather-related phenomenon, you can collect ice and snow in clean containers and use the ice and snow to help keep foods colder longer. If it is really cold, some foods, properly cased, may be able to be stored on a porch or in some other open area. Watch the thermometer so you'll be prepared if the weather warms up.

If you're in an area prone to flooding, you have special concerns regarding your food supply. If the food is not stored at a height that prevents it from contact with flood waters and there is a flood of any sort that reaches the food, you must discard a great many items and take special precautions with the rest.

Again, although it may seem wasteful, the health risk posed by flood waters is almost beyond imagining. Raw sewage, decaying tissue, chemicals and poisons – and that's just for openers when it comes to flood waters. Throw out any food that might have come in contact with flood water, anything not in waterproof containers. And the nature of waterproof containers will surprise you. *Screw caps, snap lids, pull tops and crimped lids are NOT waterproof!* An undamaged packet of **Capri Sun**, however, *is* waterproof.

Actual waterproof containers must be cleaned up before being used or returned to storage. Bacteria can accumulate under labels. Labels must be removed. Wash the cans with soap and clean water. Purify the water with the water filter that's part of your bug-out bag contents. If your filter is unavailable, take the following steps. Boil the water if you can. Whether boiling is possible or not, it is recommended that you first take some sort of cloth – like a clean T-shirt – and filter the water through this to remove sediment. Let the rest of the sediment sink to the bottom of your container and pour out the good water from the top – the remaining sediment and some water should be discarded. Then, go ahead and boil the water. If there is no facility to boil the water, the USDA recommends you add eight drops of regular household bleach per gallon. Don't use scented bleach or bleaches with additives. Shake the container to thoroughly mix in the bleach. Let the water sit for 15 minutes, at least. Now you have water clean enough to wash those contaminated canned goods, but not yet clean enough to risk drinking.

Once again, make certain all labels and price tags are removed. After washing the cans and pouches with the soap and clean water, rinse thoroughly so dirt and residual soap won't re-contaminate them. Then sanitize the cans and pouches by placing them in boiling water for two minutes. If you still can't boil, it's time for more bleach. Add one tablespoon of bleach per gallon of the cleanest water available and let sit for 15 minutes. Air dry the cans for at least one hour before opening or storing. Mark the cans and use the contents as soon as practical. If the can seems overly rusty, or there is a bulge or dent, err on the side of caution and get rid of the can and its contents before wasting soap and water on it.

The same regimen applies to pots and pans that may have been contaminated with flood waters. Wash in soap and clean water, and then use boiling water or bleach.

Remember that bottled water containers are not truly watertight, so don't drink water that has been exposed to flood waters. When Sharon and I were in high school, I knew still another army sergeant who told the story of how he'd gotten an intestinal worm of some kind that he had to have surgically removed. The story may be apocryphal. He claimed that, while posted in then West Germany, he saw a water supply marked in English "NOT POTABLE." The good sergeant thought that meant you couldn't carry the water away – as in "portable." If you don't have something like a Katadyn Pocket Filter or you can't boil the water, filter it with the T-shirt or clean rag and add eight drops of regular bleach for each gallon of water. Mix or stir and let the water stand for

30 minutes. Store the water in clean containers with covers.

Not during a flood, of course, but in preparation for other types of emergency situations, one of the first things you should do is take every clean container you've got and start filling them with water. Fill the bathtub or bathtubs with water. Open pans, too, can be filled. You won't be drinking this water as-is, but you may wind up using it for periodic toilet flushing and you may wind up boiling it or using the bleach purification methods and using the water for washing or for drinking.

One of mankind's oldest portable foods was jerky. Wild game is ideal for making jerky because it is so lean. Fatty meats have a tendency to go rancid. Certainly, jerky can be stored in a refrigerator and kept longer, but jerky – especially the commercial kind – will store for a reasonable amount of time without refrigeration, as everyone from early man to real life cowboys knew. You can make your own jerky and save lots of money over the "store bought" kind; but, either way, jerky is nourishing, tastes good and doesn't absolutely have to have refrigeration. Keep your jerky in an airtight jar or, better still, in double-seal plastic storage bags. It's great trail and survival food.

Some smoked meats can be kept without refrigeration for quite some time. One of our grandsons makes peculiar requests for Christmas presents. Or maybe he was just getting ready for a survival situation: he asked for summer sausage! We obliged with beef summer sausage – along with something more conventional, too.

Little Vienna sausages from a can, canned stew from **Dinty Moore** (first introduced in the USA in 1935) and **Castleberry's** (returning to store shelves as "American Originals"), hearty soups from **Progresso**, and the original **Spam** – which actually tastes pretty good – can be heated, of course, but can also be eaten cold. They keep and keep and are, generally, quite good for you. Let's not forget Italian, of course. **Chef Boyardee Beef Ravioli** (regular and over-stuffed) and **Campbell's** (formerly Franco-American) **Spaghettios with Meatballs** and **with Franks** is also available. Each serving of these Campbell products, for example, provides, "…a serving of vegetables, a serving of grains and at least six essential vitamins and minerals." How can you beat that?

CHAPTER 12:
MEDICAL
PREPAREDNESS

It seems that medical emergencies often come at the worst possible times. When I had my heart attack, the clock was pushing midnight. Just because you're in the middle of a disaster scenario doesn't mean the normal problems will go on hold. And, of course, elements of the disaster itself can and probably will contribute to greater and more frequent needs for medical assistance. The trouble is that during a disaster and its aftermath, whether natural or man-made, actual medical assistance may prove all but impossible for you to reach, or it may be be totally unable to reach you. You are stuck without professional help and you must rely on yourself, your nuclear family, your extended family and/or your prepared community.

In the shaping of the prepared community, you'll see, one of the important things to do is identify individual areas of expertise which can be utilized in an emergency. Perhaps most important among these specialties is medical training. It'd be great to have a vigorous retired medical doctor and his equally vigorous retired registered nurse wife living down the block, but the likelihood of that situation isn't great. You may find yourself counting your blessings that somebody over on the next block dropped out of a Red Cross First Aid Course a dozen years ago but kept the textbook.

Somewhere between those two extremes – the retired doctor/nurse team and the First Aid Course drop-out – is what you should try to have available during a disaster scenario. You can't just keep your fingers crossed.

Indeed, get somebody in your group – hopefully several somebodies – to sign up for and complete a Red Cross First Aid Course. But, some of your First Aid needs in a disaster scenario may surpass basic procedures and basic equipment. A case in point involves the parents of one of our son's best friends, a guy our son has been pals with since kindergarten close to 30 years ago. Our son's friend's parents went on a hike. The wife was bitten by a deadly poisonous snake and the husband heroically struggled to get her to medical assistance. She nearly died before recovering fully. They are nice people and quite smart. Probably, in the future, they'll do what they should have done then and carry a snake bite kit. The kits take up precious little room and are your first line of defense – after snake-proof boots – against this cause of injury or death.

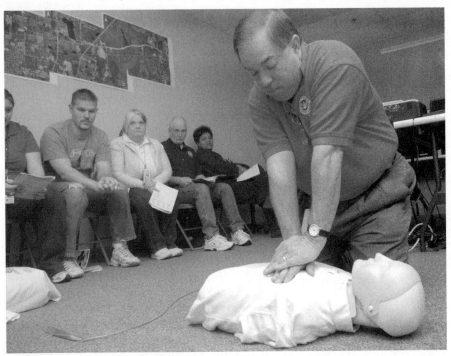

FEMA worker conducts a First Aid course in CPR. Photo courtesy FEMA News Photo

There are some books and a DVD I would recommend you investigate and consider acquiring. *Ditch Medicine*, by Hugh L. Coffee (Paladin Press, 1993), is a valuable book about undertaking serious medical procedures in less than ideal circumstances. There is a DVD of the same name. From the same publisher comes *Survival*, by Chris and Gretchen Janowsky, another excellent work. Also from Paladin is *The U.S. Army Special Forces Medical Handbook*, by Glen K. Craig. For a variety of survival skills, not just First Aid, it could be useful in a number of disaster scenarios to have a copy of *Combat Leader's Field Guide* from Stackpole Books. The 13th Edition is in a trade paperback form; my much, much earlier copy is printed in a smaller format and is intended to be carried along in a pocket or some other manner, on body. The information is just as good in the newer version and more up-to-date.

Don't just buy the books, of course. Study them so you know how to use them as references for medical procedures you or someone else may have to perform. *Taking up valuable time searching for the treatment needed after the fact could be fatal.*

Without sounding nosey, try to find out who has what chronic conditions in your extended family and your prepared community. Determine what equipment and techniques might prove useful in these specific instances. In the case of pregnancy, hope the delivery will come after the disaster has passed – hope, but don't count on it. In ages gone by, and in some parts of the world still, pregnant women just march along with the tribe, drop off to have the baby and, baby in tow, catch up to the tribe. That's not something I'd wish on anyone, however. If there are pregnancies in your nuclear family, extended family or prepared community, tactfully ascertain if any previous pregnancies evidenced complications or were C-sections. In the case of complications or C-sections, if the possibility of delivery exists within the time frame of the situation within which you find yourself embroiled, immediately start planning how this special-needs delivery will be handled.

Before the crisis, in the event you'll have a special needs delivery with which to deal, learn how to improvise a safe incubator and what to do about bilirubin, a common post-natal jaundice-like condition. You'll need some specialized equipment, and it can be rigged up. For example, with the incubator, you'll need to precisely control temperature and timing. Your extended family or prepared community medical team needs to be on top of this situation, because babies don't wait to be born at a time convenient for the rest of us.

To guard against traumatic incident, be extra cautious. If there are kerosene heaters present, for example, make certain that they are filled outside and under controlled conditions. How are you handling these units to minimize risk of burns or fire?

Any complex machinery should be practiced with, so that, under emergency conditions, when people are nervous and more prone to mistakes, risk of accident or injury will be minimized.

Safety in the industrial and military contexts is constantly reviewed and critiqued. Some of the activities that you, your nuclear family, the extended family and the prepared community may have to perform in a disaster and its aftermath are not unlike operating dangerous equipment or undertaking hazardous tasks.

The concept of disaster preparedness drills has already been touched upon. Communities of all sizes have such drills in which local police, fire and emergency personnel work in concert with hospitals and other organizations, trying to iron out the kinks in disaster response planning. Your nuclear family, extended family and prepared community can do the same. Injuries are tagged – suspected broken collar bone, sucking chest wound, etc. – and the injured are triaged, and then moved on for simulated care. This training can kick in if and when the real thing happens. A rule for this type of treatment by lay personnel is to do nothing more than needs to be done. Don't borrow trouble. You'll have all you can use and more as it is.

In the event someone should get shot, by accident or design, bullet wounds demand special attention beyond what you see in the movies. Think in terms of the word "infection." Unless a bullet enters a naked portion of the body – like a hand – it will not only take all the dirt and powder residue attendant to the bullet itself, but will also push into the wound bits of the wounded person's clothing or any object the bullet may have passed through. When you are treating a bullet wound, you must contend with this. Remember the old military dictum: **"Stop the bleeding! Protect the wound! Treat for shock!"** Don't forget that. If you don't treat for shock, even less than fatal wounds can prove fatal. If you don't properly guard against infection, your "patient" may become seriously ill or die.

The normal things of life may be a little more difficult or a lot more difficult in a disaster and its aftermath. Remember that water pumping stations are computer-controlled and run on electricity. Most stations will have generators, but generators need to be fueled and serviced. If the generator stops, water pressure will fail. Not only can this mean the supply of potable drinking water will "dry up," but water for bathing, brushing teeth and – very importantly – sanitary needs won't be available, either. Chemical toilets can be acquired, of course, and normal toilets will work if you can spare the water to flush them, by-passing the flush tank or filling the flush tank from a bucket. If there's any chance sewer pipes may be ruptured or compromised by flooding or if water is in short supply, two techniques can be tried alternative to flushing. First, you can remove the seat from a toilet and place the seat on a bucket. The seat feels familiar and the bucket's contents can be disposed of (Be careful where and how). The other technique allows use of the toilet almost normally. Shut off the water supply and flush the toilet. If possible, let the bowl air dry. Place a sturdy plastic trash bag inside the bowl and close the seat over it. When you need to or feel you should, lift the seat and close the bag and take it out to be properly disposed of, after placing the first bag inside a clean second bag. Replace the bag you had in the toilet.

Latrines can be dug, but this must be undertaken with care. A slit trench is nothing more than a hole in the ground that you straddle. This would be a radical step in an even moderately urbanized area and must be carefully considered. Any disposal of human waste contaminated water – brown water– must occur downstream, as it were, of any possible source of potable water. It's wise to make certain that water used for hand washing or other non-human waste-related purposes – grey water – is safely taken care of as well.

If you live in a rural area or close to one and have a well, it likely uses either an above ground jet pump or a submersible pump. The jet pump works like a straw and is most commonly used with ground water that is not too terribly far below the surface. If you must draw water from more than 25 feet below the surface, you'll need a double drop jet pump or, for best results, a submersible. But, unless you have the old kind of well you see in western movies that utilizes a bucket, or unless your well is powered by a windmill or solar cells, you'll need electricity from the power company or a generator to get your water out of it.

For bathing, if you're unable to run water through your pipes, you can use buckets of water and just stand and "shower" in the bathtub or shower enclosure. It's like taking a shower in a travel trailer with the water coming out of the holding tank. You get wet and you soap up and you rinse. Water is poured from the bucket only when you are getting wet and rinsing. You'd be surprised how little water that system uses in comparison to a standard shower. You'll probably want to warm the water before pouring it on your naked body. To do that in the out doors, you can use a sun shower. There are various types, some solar-powered, some battery-powered. Some use propane to heat the water and some have tent-like enclosures so you have a warm shower and privacy. These are camping-related products, so continuous use over a protracted period of time might wear them out rather quickly. The point is, personal hygiene is vital to continued good health and, so long as you've got the clean water or water that can be made clean, you can stay showered.

Even if you have to evacuate an area, try your best to have at least one change of outer clothes and a couple of sets of underwear and socks. You can catch infections from dirty underwear and dirty socks aren't conducive to good foot health. You need your feet in good shape in order to walk, of course, and blistered or cracked skin on your feet will not only make you miserable, it will eventually keep you from moving effectively.

In the staying clean department, remember the importance of soap and hand sanitizer. Viruses enter the body through the nasal passages and tear ducts. They get to the nasal passages and tear ducts primarily through rubbing eyes and picking noses. **Don't spread colds or viruses!** Hygiene can be one of the first things to go when just staying alive is suddenly a challenge.

Establish medical protocols within your group and stick to them, unless you find something to do that is even more effective. For example, any open wound of any size must be cleaned and kept clean and covered with some sort of dressing.

Keep food in clean, closed containers. If it must be refrigerated to be safe and cannot be refrigerated, it's not safe. Don't eat or drink something you suspect to be unsafe. If you are miserable because you are hungry, you'll feel even worse with stomach cramps, nausea and diarrhea heaped on. Water that does not come out of a securely closed sanitary container is suspect and must be boiled – brought to a rolling boil – for at least three to five minutes, then allowed to cool before use. Cooking implements and eating utensils need to be washed. If most of what you plan to eat will be from sealed containers, warmed as required and the containers discarded, do yourself a favor and stick to disposable plastic wear. Dispose of such things properly, of course. Worry about the environmental impact of plastic forks and spoons and paper plates later.

Keep an eye on each other for changes in physical or mental stability and try to head off these debilitating conditions before they go too far. Encourage people to keep up their appetites and continue with physical fitness regimens as much as possible. If sports can be organized – even just tossing a ball around or flying a Frisbee – it will promote mental and physical health.

In a bad situation, it is easy to so focus on the "now" that you forget there will be a "later." Certainly things can always get worse, but there's usually a pretty good chance that things might change for the better, too. In a disaster survival situation, you must maintain your own spirits and help to raise the spirits of those with whom you interact. Don't be obviously overenthusiastic or no one will pay attention to your attempts at positivity. Try to realistically look on the brighter side of things. Although such situations lend themselves wonderfully well to depression, it's counter-productive and there's really no time for it, anyway.

CHAPTER 13:
GENERATORS AND BATTERIES

The importance of light and electricity to power some of the basic necessities is never truly appreciated until they're absent. Most of us, certainly, have experienced a temporary power outage lasting minutes or even hours. Rarely, outages will last days. If you keep your refrigerator and freezer closed, opening them only for as brief a period as possible in order to grab something, you are looking at four hours of shelf life for things like meat and eggs and dairy products, according to the United States Department of Agriculture. If you have a separate freezer and it is half full, you'll have 24 hours. A full freezer will be safe for as much as 48 hours. The United States Department of Agriculture also recommends having a thermometer for testing food. Frozen food should be at 0° Fahrenheit or below, while fresh refrigerated food should be at 40° F or below. According to the USDA, those are the limits. USDA also recommends locating a source for block ice – cubes would probably help in a pinch – or dry ice that can be placed in the refrigerator or the freezer to keep the temperature lower longer.

Having a generator available that can run refrigerators and freezers is the only long-term solution for a crisis that may last several days or a week or longer. The prepared community can pool resources to secure a sufficient number of generators to power the prepared community's cold food storage needs and some lighting and periodic internet use for news and other information about the crisis.

Generators are available from a wide range of sources. The **Honda Handi Inverter EU3000i** is an excellent example. Introduced in the summer of 2009, it is Honda's lightest-weight inverter generator and easily lifted by a man of modest strength or a strong woman. Two people of either sex could easily manipulate it. There are offset handles to facilitate lifting and it has wheels for rolling it rather than lifting it at all. Gasoline powered, it has a 3000-watt capacity and it is quiet to run.

Ahern wheeling the Honda generator, which is quite easy to move about.

Let's consider that 3000-watt capacity. An energy-efficient refrigerator or freezer, according to Honda's figures, requires 1200 watts of start-up power. Running power is vastly lower, but remember that refrigerators continually re-start to maintain temperature. So, if both a refrigerator and a freezer were doing that simultaneously, you'd have very little wattage left for a safe margin. You can run some lights. But it won't kill the food in the freezer if you disconnect the freezer from the generator for several hours a day, thus giving you plenty of power, not only for running some lights, but for running your comput-

The Honda generator's controls are simple and straightforward.

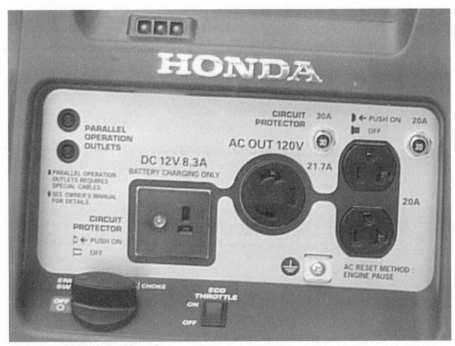

Close-up of the control panel.

Note control panel and fuel inlet.

Left side and right side (shown below).

er and monitor, or a radio or a television. Such electrical power management will allow you to keep rechargeable flashlights and similar low-wattage items fully charged and ready to go.

We found the instruction manual accompanying the Honda EU3000i to give in-depth coverage of all the features the firm's legal staff apparently wanted included. We also found the website (www.hondapowerequipment.com/generators) to be extremely helpful.

Generators come in various wattage ranges, and this affects the size and weight of the unit, as well as its cost. With the Honda EU3000i, a state-of-the-art unit to be sure, you get around eight hours of run time for well under two gallons of gasoline. Wouldn't it be great if you could run your car or truck for over seven hours with gas economy like that?

You will need a professional, licensed electrician to install a transfer switch for you. As Honda explains it, the transfer switch will be located near your electrical box and connected to several circuits you select. When the power goes off, the transfer switch must be set to generator power; and, when the power is restored, the transfer switch must be set once again, thus blocking the generator. Honda's **UTS (Universal Transfer Switch)** is programmable and makes it faster and more efficient for you to switch over to generator power. It's a great system and a safe system, too, preventing back-feed from your generator into the power lines and thus guarding against accidents. The transfer switch also prevents back-feed from the power lines into your generator. Such back-feed can destroy your generator and could even start a fire. The properly installed and properly functioning transfer switch, whether the automatic UTS type or the manual type, positively precludes both the power from the utility company and your generator from running at the same time.

There are three common types of generators as concerns fuel. There are those that run on gasoline and those that use diesel. There are also propane (LP and natural gas) powered generators. The popular wisdom on this subject is that gasoline generators are generally easier to run. Diesel generators get better "mileage" and they last longer than those that use gasoline. Propane

Ahern carrying the Honda generator, which weighs only 70 lbs. without fuel and oil.

generators, running on a twenty-pounder, are most convenient to use and kinder to the environment. So the general rule of thumb is this: Get a diesel-powered generator if you plan on long term, continuous use; a gasoline-powered generator if convenient periodic shorter term use is all you need; or a propane-powered generator for unmatched ease and safety of refueling and convenient storage of fuel. For our purposes, unless the manmade or natural disaster so overwhelms civilization that we might take years to recover, if ever, the gasoline- or propane-powered generator will likely be all you'll need.

Of course, if you're seriously into conservation or just resent paying the utility company for your electricity, you can use batteries to store power you generate through solar panels or wind power. The initial cost is high, but your electricity will be free and some power companies will buy excess power you generate over and above your own needs. If you were to go through a prolonged period of heavily overcast skies or a period where winds were calm for an inordinate amount of time, you still shouldn't have a problem, because storage batteries should have enough charge to sustain you. If you can afford the solar or wind equipment, you can probably afford a good generator as an emergency backup. In a crisis, you would have all the electricity you normally have and there would be little or no disruption.

Carefully assess your power needs in an emergency, but do so well before the emergency is upon you. If you can, you may very well wish to choose solar power or wind power, wholly or partially, since even partial independence from the power grid will eventually save money and will assure you of electrical power under virtually any conceivable conditions. Assessing your needs will enable you to accurately determine which size and fuel-style of generator will meet your needs and your budget.

You'll note that, up to this point, there has been no discussion here of hydro-electric emergency power. Drought and other phenomena can impact rivers and streams, of course, and affect your electrical power. Yet if you have a reliable water source and are willing to back it up with an emergency generator – just in case – a fast-running stream can be just the ticket. You need more than a waterwheel, but for a direct current (DC) system, the power from which can be converted to run alternating current (AC) equipment, a relatively modest number of gallons per minute is enough to run a modest-sized energy efficient home. Setting up the DC system – you can buy the parts and the plans – and seeing to its maintenance will enable you to have clean energy without using fossil fuels or paying the power company. In a perfect world, you'd build your house by a fast-running stream, install solar panels in your roof and have some wind power for good measure. Any or all of these systems are pretty disruption-proof, as long as the weather generally co-operates and you've got your storage batteries online.

Self-sufficiency with electrical power is the ideal situation.

When there is no external electrical power available, of course, and candles won't do the job, most of us will turn to battery-operated devices.

Our adult children must think I have a flashlight fetish. Well, maybe I do. I keep a three D-Cell **MagLite** next to the bed. I keep a re-chargeable MagLite near the front door for walking the dog at night. I carry a **SureFire light** of some sort every time I think I might be out at night or in a portion of a building where there are no windows. I keep a **Photon Micro Light** on the ring with my car keys.

Although I've got a backup re-chargeable battery, I've been using the same re-chargeable battery I started with in my re-chargeable MagLite when I originally acquired it in 1999. I use it essentially every day.

For regular batteries – and this is purely personal preference – I use **Dura-Cells** whenever possible, as I have found them to last a ridiculously long time, provide reliable power and go bad and start sweating acid virtually not at all. We unwittingly conducted an experiment involving a Coleman lantern. We had an eight D-Cell model that we acquired in 1999. We placed four Dura-Cell batteries in the Coleman lantern and four of another well-respected brand in the lantern, as well.

About five or six years ago, the switch got turned the wrong way and the lantern would no longer work. Then, early in the spring of 2009, I thought about the lantern and asked a friend who's quite the handy man – it's one of his businesses – to take a look at it. The first thing he did was open the base to check the condition of the batteries. The four original "other brand" batteries had corroded and leaked acid. The four Dura-Cells had not. I've actually had Dura-Cells in low-use flashlights for 10 years or longer and they still work and haven't gone bad. No, I don't own stock in the company.

In my SureFire lights, of course, I use SureFire's private-brand lithium batteries. They work just great. I'm a SureFire fan.

I'm not really into stumbling around in the dark, although I have always

From left: a battery-operated Coleman lantern, a lantern that runs on Coleman fuel and the Coleman fuel container, a propane-powered Coleman lantern with reflector to direct the light, and an antique kerosene lamp that's still functional.

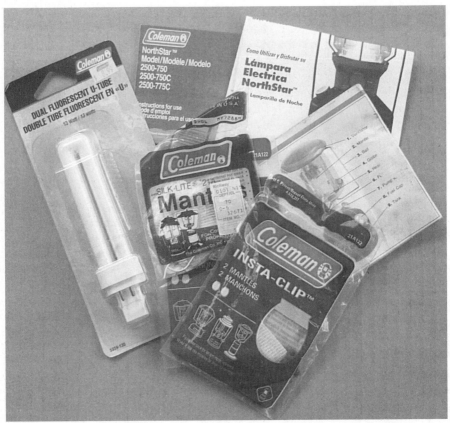

An assortment of spare parts and instructions for the Coleman light products.

had better-than-average night vision and still do. I'll stick to my flashlights, regardless of what our children and grandchildren think.

Battery-operated emergency lighting is not, however, the only other choice besides a candle or candles. The most famous Coleman product is THE **Coleman Lantern**. Its appearance has changed considerably over the century since its inception, but the reliability and ease of operation which made Admiral Byrd take Coleman lanterns to the South Pole have stayed the same. It uses propane, available under the Coleman label as a proprietary Coleman product and under other brands as well. The Coleman cylinders contain 16.4 ounces apiece of liquid propane (LP) gas. LP gas is available pretty much everywhere. The familiar canisters associated with backyard grills are the 4.73-gallon "twenty-pounders." "Distribution trees," basically three-way adapter lines, are available that allow you to run up to three propane appliances off of one twenty-pounder.

Generators to substitute for electricity from your utility company or battery-powered flashlights or the familiar Coleman lantern – the wise person will have more than one or all of these choices available in the event of a disaster that throws us into the dark.

CHAPTER 14:
SURVIVAL WEAPONS

Ahern is always armed where legal, even at home. This is Ahern's Seecamp .32 and vintage front pocket holster.

In emergency situations, law enforcement capabilities are typically stretched to their maximum and beyond, resulting in slower responses to calls for help – if such responses come at all. During a calamity, civil disobedience and criminal activity in general will often be at heightened levels. Sadly, those who are prepared for an emergency situation may well find themselves preyed upon by those who are not.

Weapons policies must be carefully considered and formulated in order to counter these threats. The objective is the maintenance of security for the nuclear family, extended family and prepared community group while avoiding the appearance of some sort of group that is armed and looking for trouble – when trouble is what all concerned wish to avoid. Remember that these days, many persons are extremely fearful of weapons and distrust persons who have them. This has been bred into our common consciousness by some media and education elements.

Adding to this potential distrust is the fact that, due to our largely urbanized society, fewer people grow up using firearms for hunting and other forms of recreation. Humankind tends to distrust or even fear that which it does not understand or with which it is unfamiliar. About 30 years ago, we were going on a trip and asked Sharon's mom and dad to keep a few guns for us, among them an AR-15. It was empty, of course. But, Sharon and I were certain (and still are) that her mom expected the AR-15 to somehow load itself, chamber a round and shoot her.

If you are a person who finds firearms and firearms training abhorrent, please skip over to the next chapter and good luck to you. God willing, you won't need the luck part.

If you have no knowledge of firearms and firearms use, yet realize the necessity of self-protection all or at least some of the time, find someone who does have this knowledge – someone who seems responsible and whom you would trust for other important purposes. If you know of no such person, don't despair. Usually, a gun shop or gun club in your area can recommend some possibilities to you. Gun people are usually very friendly.

If you have knowledge of firearms or choose to acquire that skill set, I present some suggestions. Remember that you are trying to avoid the armed and dangerous look to those good people who, like you, are armed and those other good people, who are not. We don't want to scare people unless they are trying to hurt us; then, we frighten them with our resolve and the weaponry to back it up.

Any weapon is better than no weapon at all. We have a relative who doesn't trust himself to have a gun around. When Y2K was coming upon us, we were finally able to convince him to borrow an aluminum softball bat. It would have been better than nothing and he was comfortable with it.

The Rifle

When it comes to rifles, the smartest choices will be those rifles that operate semi-automatically. This type of rifle automatically chambers the next round

after a round is fired, but the trigger must be depressed for each round fired. This is different from true automatics (i.e., machineguns), which continue firing as long as the trigger is held back, until the ammunition in the magazine is exhausted. Semi-automatic rifles are fed by some type of removable box magazine. This does not necessarily mean a "black" rifle, but it might. A standard **Ruger Mini-14 Ranch Rifle** in .223 Remington (the slightly down-loaded civilian counterpart of the 5.56X45mm U.S. military round) is a fine choice, the caliber a common one and the rifles themselves equipped with a nice looking hardwood stock that

Ahern always keeps at least two handguns, a knife, a flashlight and a telephone next to the bed. The handgun at left is a Detonics CombatMaster .45 and the revolver by the telephone is a .38 Special S&W Model 640 with Crimson Trace LaserGrips.

is a warm brown color and projects a "sporting" air rather than a military one.

If you want a caliber with more power, the same rifle is available as the **Mini 30**, in 7.62 X39 Russian, sometimes known as .30 Russian. For my own purposes, I would have no qualms with the "black" rifle image conveyed by an **AR-15** or a semi-automatic **AK-47**, but neighbors and others who are afraid of or prejudiced against guns probably would – if I had such neighbors.

After the .223 and the 7.62X39, the third caliber I would recommend in a semi-automatic rifle is 7.62X51 NATO, also known as .308 Winchester. The **Heckler & Koch HK-91** was a superb rifle, so superb you will likely be unable to find anyone selling one. If you do, it will be expensive. There are other rifles in the caliber that are also semi-automatics, the **Belgian FN-FAL** (Fabrique Nationale – Fusil Automatique Leguerre) being one of the more well-known.

A less expensive but truly excellent rifle in 7.62 NATO is the Spanish-made

CETME, also a battle rifle. This is a personal favorite, well-made, accurate and ruggedly built.

A fine .308 is available from Springfield Armory as the **M1A**. It is a civilian, semi-auto only version of the M-14 rifle, the U.S. service rifle that was phased out in favor of the M-16 series rifles of the Viet Nam era forward. Most semi-automatic hunting arms in this caliber will have magazines that hold only five or 10 shots, which is much less than the capacity of a military-style rifle. Also, most hunting rifles of this type aren't built to take the heat build-up of sustained firing that a military sporter can handle.

Of all three calibers I'm recommending for this application, .223 cartridges have the lightest weight. Therefore, if you must evacuate but will still be armed, you can carry more ammunition. .308 Winchester cartridges are the heaviest, but in terms of power they're ideal if evacuation is impossible – and that would be a tough thing to determine.

The best compromise might be the 7.62 Russian, weighing somewhere in between the .223 and the .308 per cartridge. The .223 and .308 are generally accepted as having greater long range accuracy potential than 7.62 Russian. For practical accuracy at practical ranges, though, that's splitting hairs. Of the three rounds, .308 will reach out with greatest authority at longer ranges.

If rifles might be pressed into service to bring down a deer to supplement the larder, full metal case (FMC) military-style ammunition is less than ideal. (FMC ammunition has no lead exposed at the tip, so it doesn't readily expand inside an animal's body, making it a poor choice for hunting purposes.) The .308 is certainly up to the task of taking a deer, and a wide range of ammunition is available in this caliber, some of which is more more suitable for hunting than FMC. The 7.62 Russian is also capable of taking deer, but, again, the typical FMC ammunition shouldn't be used for this except in a pinch. The .223 is legal for deer in many areas, but as was true of the .308 and the 7.62X39, you won't want to use military-style FMC bullets for taking deer. Acquire a modest amount of cartridges with bullet designs more suitable to use on game – softpoints, for example (If you don't know what a softpoint is, visit your local gun store and ask the counter attendant to show you some). If you do choose the .223, you must be very adept at bullet placement – the neck or head, typically – in order to ensure a humane kill rather than a torturous injury for the animal.

The Ruger Ranch Rifle comes standard with a five-round removable box magazine. This is ideal for hunting, but far less than ideal for defensive purposes. As this is written, Ruger has at last started releasing 20-round magazines bearing its own marque, rather than forcing consumers to purchase aftermarket magazines. Depending on the maker, aftermarket magazines can be very good – or not so good. Whatever you wind up with, make certain your magazines are properly working specimens.

Depending on where you live, there may be certain firearms-related restrictions. High-capacity magazines may be banned in your city or state, for example. It is your responsibility to become familiar with all laws governing your ownership and use of firearms.

From top, a folding stock Ruger Mini 14 in .223, a CETME .308 and a WASR AK-47 in 7.62X39 with folding stock, all semi-automatic and representing the three most available calibers favored by military and police.

Magazines and Ammunition

If you already own or have decided to acquire a magazine-fed semi-automatic rifle, you will want more than one magazine. In many areas, magazine capacity *for general use* is not limited, but magazine capacity *for hunting use* may be. Although Georgia makes no such restrictions regarding rifles, I have a five-round magazine for my semi-automatic WASR AK-47 anyway. Typically, AK-47 magazines are 30-round capacity.

Note my use of the term "semi-automatic" when referencing my AK-47 type rifle. *Do not, under any circumstances, attempt to illegally alter a weapon to selective or full-auto fire, or to acquire one so altered.* Legality issues aside, many

such weapons will likely be gun-smithed rather poorly. And, even if that is not the case, although shooting someone else's automatic/selective-fire weapons at a range or under some other fully legal circumstance is a lot of fun, such weapons can eat up ammunition. Give the untrained or unfamiliar person a selective fire weapon set to full-auto and the shooter will frequently blow through much of the entire magazine with one pull of the trigger. You don't use automatic weapons like that. In the unlikely event that you'll have to make a "drug store stand" in defense of your nuclear family, extended family or prepared community, it must be remembered that you are not in a war movie. No trucks will be coming up from behind your lines to off-load cases of ammunition and, if you burn out a barrel, you've got a "broken" rifle that's not going to be fixed by the unit armorer.

Once again, however, any weapon is better than none at all. If you collect NFA (National Firearms Act) weapons capable of automatic fire, then that may be all you've got. Similarly, a bolt action or lever action (in a rifle caliber, rather than a handgun caliber) deer rifle might be all you have available. A .30-30 Winchester or Marlin lever action (the type seen in countless westerns and seen in pickup trucks all over much of rural America) is perfectly fine, if that's what you've got.

If the only rifle you own is a .22, learn how to be a pinpoint marksman with it and stock up on ammunition. My two favorite .22 rifles are the **Ruger 10/22** (for which aftermarket high-capacity magazines are available, as of this writing) and the **Henry U.S. Survival Rifle**.

As this is written, the USA has just undergone a period during which certain firearms and quite a number of ammunition calibers were in extremely short supply, a period from which the nation seems to be emerging. In a crisis situation, even if gun shops and other establishments selling ammunition were to remain open, ammunition, milk, baby food and formula, canned goods, cigarettes and beer would be some of the first items to disappear from the shelves.

A Cimarron Arms hoop lever Model 92 in .45 Colt and a Glenfield .30-30.

The hoop lever Cimarron in .45 Colt and a Cimarron single action revolver in the same caliber make great gear for Cowboy Action shooting, but can be pressed into emergency service if needed.

Assess your needs and try to stockpile what you can in your caliber or calibers of choice. You won't need thousands of rounds, but hundreds of rounds could prove useful. In a more protracted crisis, .22 Long Rifle (.22 LR) ammunition and other calibers, along with 12 gauge shotgun shells, could prove immensely convenient as trading gear. The .22 LR is so useful because it can be employed to pot small game or dispatch vermin and, because of its light weight, large amounts of this ammunition can be easily portable.

As concerns ammunition acquisition, it is well to remember that, in certain disaster scenarios, gun and ammunition sales will be temporarily suspended by whatever authority feels it has the right or duty to do so. My wife and I lived in the Chicago area during some of the more serious civil unrest of the late 1960s. Almost immediately, the sale of all firearms and ammunition in the city (there were still some few legal firearms retailers in Chicago in those days) were curtailed by executive order from the Mayor's office.

Handguns

Although I am personally a great supporter of handgun ownership, if budgetary or other concerns must keep your firearm acquisitions to a minimum, a rifle is your best choice for a defensive scenario. Shotguns have the reputation among many shooters and non-shooters of being the perfect weapon for self-defense in times of civil disorder. My personal opinion is that the typical shotgunner will have to be too close to a hostile person or group for accurate shot placement. If you have the luxury of having several firearms available to you, certainly a good 12 gauge shotgun – I like a pump rather than a semi-automatic – is a fine component of your defensive equipment inventory. **Remington's old standby 870** is hard to beat. The sound of a pump shotgun being racked – that "chunk-chunk" – will possibly deter some attackers. It's worth a try, anyway.

In the vast majority of disaster scenarios, you will probably not need a weapon for anything more than the "comfort factor" of knowing it is there and ready to be pressed into service, should such a situation become reality. For that reason – the comfort factor – I would suggest that the firearm or at least one firearm should be quite portable, of handy size and not

(below) Ahern with the Remington 870.

(bottom) A Remington 12-gauge 870 shotgun with a sling loaded with slugs and spare ammo on the buttstock and an extended magazine. A bit old-fashioned, but still one of the finest shotguns of the type.

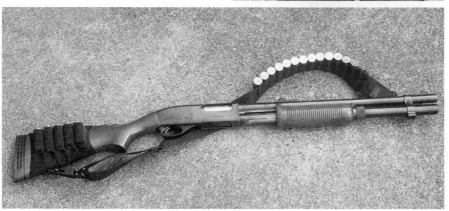

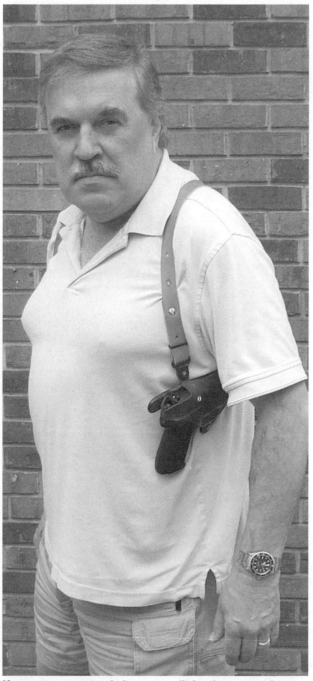

If you carry a concealed weapon all the time or you just want to plan for an emergency, a balanced should rig such as this old Galco Miami Classic for the SIG 229 can be quite convenient.

terribly heavy. The principal reason for a handgun in such a situation is that it can be worn and does not have to be set down and left unattended and, perhaps, out of reach when needed.

Having weapons available demands the observance of basic safety rules which all shooters know. Such common practices should certainly be more rigorously adhered to in a crisis situation, when medical help might be delayed at best.

Among defensive handgun calibers, the top choices are **.45 ACP, .40 S&W, .357 Magnum, .357 SIG and 9X19 mm Parabellum**. If all you own is a .38 Special revolver or a .38 Super semiautomatic or a .45 Colt cowboy-style six shooter, such a situation is not a disaster. Handguns in .38 Special, .38 Super or .45 Colt caliber are more than adequate to most defensive needs; it's just that the other calibers are better suited

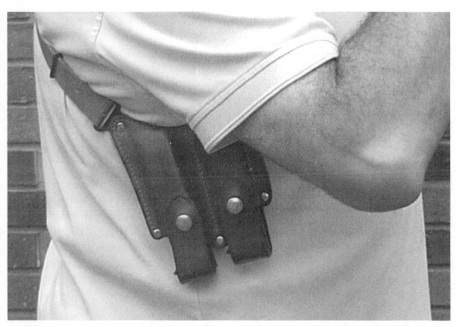

The offside of the shoulder holster Ahern wears carries two spare magazines for the pistol.

to the task and ammunition for them might be more easily found when you need it. Which handgun caliber is most common? Depends on where you live. The 9mm Parabellum is, as this is written, reportedly the most commonly encountered police handgun caliber in the United States. The .40 S&W is also extremely popular. The .357 SIG is an excellent round, but it's less common than the 9mm or the .40. The .357 Magnum is a revolver round, of course, and .38 Special ammunition can be fired from a .357 Magnum revolver (but not conversely) when necessary or desired.

Even the more modern revolvers with seven- or eight-round cylinders carry perhaps half as many rounds as the larger capacity semi-automatics. .45 ACP ("Automatic Colt Pistol," the original designation) ammunition is heavier than a great many pistol cartridges, and magazine capacity in the firearms that chamber .45 is usually less than for comparably-sized firearms in many of the other calibers. If weight is a factor, which it could certainly be if the circumstances associated with a particular disaster require evacuation or movement, the .45 ACP might not be your best choice.

Reloading one's own ammunition can be a pleasant pastime and can save considerable sums of money, too. We have a **Dillon Model RL 550B Reloading Machine**. If you elect to get into reloading, of course, you'll still have to acquire components – primers, powder and bullets – but you save money overall in terms of case cost and someone else's labor to assemble the components into loaded cartridges. Reloading can involve automatic machines that are quite complex, or they can be very simple devices for reloading one cartridge at a time.

Which one you choose depends on the amount of ammunition you want to have on hand and how much time and money you're willing to invest in reloading.

Reloading manuals exist that cover all aspects of reloading. The common wisdom, to which one should always adhere, is to work one's way up in power, never starting at maximum performance loads. This is a safety concern, for you, those around you and the weapon itself.

Reloading is nothing new. In the frontier days, ammunition was expensive and sometimes hard to come by – rather like modern times, in that regard. Reloading fired cases to manufacture fresh ammunition was a common and practical practice. Another aspect of reloading, but better suited to other firearms-related tasks than those of concern here, is making one's own lead bullets by melting the metal, pouring the molten metal into a mold – known as "casting" – and using these as the bullet. In a long-term primitive survival context, there is probably no better firearm than a flintlock rifle. The true primitive rifleman can, if need be, mine his own flint and lead and the chemicals for his black powder. That might be a fun activity, but it is not at all practical for most disaster survival scenarios.

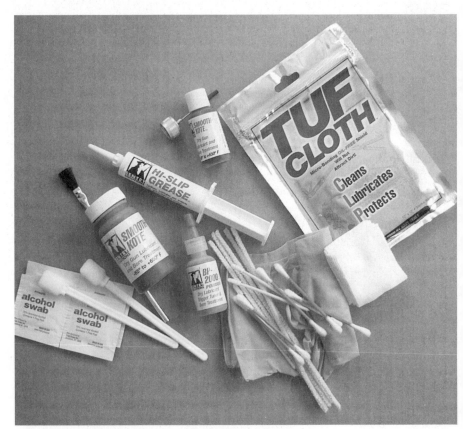

Some cleaning accessories for your firearm maintenance.

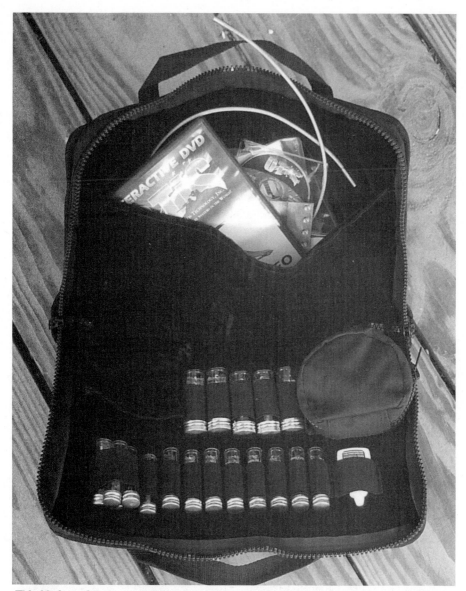

This kit from Otis is as complete as anyone could wish in terms of any normal firearm maintenance.

As mentioned in the chapter relating to the assembly of an individual disaster preparedness kit, every responsible adult should have at his or her disposal a reliable and well-crafted locking-blade folding knife unless entering into premises where such knives are prohibited – such as boarding an airplane or entering a Federal building. Similarly, in the growing number of states where shall-issue concealed carry permits are available, every adult of sound mind and adequate health who has no moral, philosophical or religious bias against weapons and being armed, should have a firearm readily available 24/7, where legally permissible.

I am very "into" guns, as the perceptive reader might deduce. I am always armed, where legally permissible. When I'm sitting down watching FOX News on television at night, there's a serious semi-automatic pistol on the coffee table. I don't even have to stand up to get it. Although not a disaster situation, per se, a home invasion is disastrous and, if manmade disasters become the order of the day, home invasions will only increase.

When I relax, I like to really relax. That means I'm prepared for whatever contingency might befall me. Along with that pistol, there's a cellular telephone, a good knife in my pocket and a giant economy-sized fire extinguisher that is three steps away, and a full-size police-style flashlight. And that's saying nothing about our courageous Honey the Wonderdog.

By this time, you might ask my personal choices in firearms for this application. I'll keep them simple. Although I have other rifles better suited for other tasks, my **WASR AK-47 with folding stock and Crimson Trace LaserGrips** forward pistol grip and a goodly number of 30-round magazines would be my first choice. As to handguns, I'm terribly biased in favor of the **Detonics single**

Three top handguns to Ahern's way of thinking for the prepared individual: SIG 229 in .40 S&W (spare .357 SIG barrel and .22 LR conversion kit kept in reserve), Detonics USA 9-11-01 in .45 ACP and Glock 22 in .40 S&W, with SureFire light and Crimson Trace LaserGrip.

The Glock, with Crimson Trace LaserGrip and SureFire light, also has night sights and is a perfect choice for this application.

action 1911-style .45 autos. Yet if I were in a static defensive mode with my nuclear family or extended family, I'd opt either for a **SIG 229 pistol in .40 S&W** or a **Glock Model 22 pistol** in the same caliber. Both have Crimson Trace LaserGrips and their much higher magazine capacity cannot be ignored.

I'll close this chapter with a firearm literally perfect for many disaster preparedness applications, and that's the unique **Henry Repeating Arms U.S. Survival .22 Rifle**. The firearm is, as noted, a rifle, but it's a rifle that disassembles to store its barrel in a compartment inside its buttstock. The latest version of this very handy rifle (as this is written) will allow one loaded eight-round .22 Long Rifle magazine seated in the receiver component and two loaded eight-round spare magazines nested within the stock as well. The receiver, magazines and barrel can be sealed within the buttstock with a tightly fitting rubber butt pad/cap, which guards against water. This is an important consideration, since the gun will float, whether assembled or disassembled. Where legal to do so and economically practical, I cannot see any reason why one would not keep such a rifle in every regularly-used vehicle.

I'm reminded of a story the late Charlton Heston recounted in his writings from his experiences during the civil dislocation which took place in Los Angeles during 1992. Some members of the entertainment community, who had assailed Heston's beliefs in the right to keep and bear arms and eschewed firearms ownership for themselves, came to him, hoping to borrow a weapon with which to guard home and family because police response had been strained by the sheer volume of violence.

Coming face to face with reality can have such a sobering effect on any of us.

CHAPTER 15:
CONVEYANCES, VEHICLES AND VEHICULAR SURVIVAL KITS

The subject of vehicles can center on the vehicles themselves, how they are used, or what they contain. All three aspects are important in the context of disaster preparedness and survival.

If money were no object – such a silly idea! – what would your ultimate "ready for anything" vehicle be? That's all individual preference. For example,

A pickup truck is possibly the ideal vehicle in a post disaster scenario involving evacuation, if you have the means to protect the load from the elements.

I'd take a **Chevy or GMC Suburban** outfitted with four wheel drive and the largest engine available and an auxiliary gas tank to help feed it. Sharon and I drove a Suburban with a 454 V8 for lots of years. I rarely become passionate over a vehicle, but the Suburban driven by Pierce Brosnan's character in the terrific adventure film *Dante's Peak* was magnificent – right down to the snorkel to keep the air supply going to the fuel injection system when the vehicle was in high water.

Most of us will settle for what we've got sitting at the curb or in the driveway or garage.

Whatever vehicle or vehicles you have available to you which could conceivably be a part of your disaster and/or post disaster survival planning need to be brought to a condition of peak efficiency and kept that way through regular maintenance on a sensible schedule. I get an oil change about every 3000 miles. Some recommend going more miles between changes and that might be fine under normal circumstances. Let's say you go close to the maximum some recommend with synthetic oil with certain cars under the easiest driving

One of the primary rules of disaster driving: the water is ALWAYS deeper than it looks.
Photo courtesy FEMA News Photo

conditions. That's 10,000 miles. For many cars, some would recommend 7500 miles between oil changes. Three thousand, however, is the old rule of thumb. The reason I stick with that figure is because, in an emergency, I'd be able to get quite a few more miles before the oil in the crankcase turns to sludge. If I doubled my usual oil change schedule, in a situation where I had to rely on my vehicle for hard service, I might discover I'd pushed the envelope too far.

The truly important consideration is this: If you get to the very limit of the vehicle's performance capabilities just as something truly bad occurs, what then? You want to be prepared.

Not just **oil**, of course, but all **fluids and filters** should be checked and changed periodically. In my experience, **fuel filters** are rarely changed, for example, but should be. All hoses and belts need to be checked and changed as required. Remember that modern serpentine belts are very specialized from vehicle to vehicle and the chance of finding just the one you need in an emergency could be remote. Serpentine belts, too, are comparatively expensive.

You need to make a **nutrition survival kit** for your car. First of all, try to get

a shop manual for the subject vehicle. After securing this, even if you know something between nothing and comparatively little about vehicles, try to make a list of questions. Check the internet as you start to search for answers and better questions. Even if you have to pay the hourly rate, sit down with a trusted mechanic who knows your vehicle and get answers to those questions. If you are a ten-thumbed klutz when it comes to automotive maintenance, you'll be surprised at how easily you can change an air filter or what have you when you really need to and know the task. Secure spare bulbs, belts, hoses and hose clamps and, if possible, ask if there's any special trick to changing this item or that. On our car, for example, in order to replace the bulb for the front directional signals, there's an entire small assembly that needs to be accessed. But it's really easy to do.

With certain **bulbs** (halogens, for example), touching the contact portion of the bulb itself can render the entire bulb useless. Learn about these things. Find out what special tools – both the tools and their sizes – you would need for any of this comparatively simple maintenance.

Have the **tires** checked periodically and, just for ordinary safety, if they are going bad, have them replaced if at all possible. If money is an issue, as it certainly can be as this is written, you can scout around for sources selling used but serviceable tires. Maybe the used set of tires will only make it for 10,000 miles or so, but the tires only cost $10 to $20 each, installed. That beats driving on dangerously balding tires with the steel belts showing – especially in an emergency.

If you have a vehicle with the little donut spare, give serious consideration to finding a spare wheel at a junk yard and having a real tire mounted. This may take up some valuable room in the vehicle, but could well prove worth it. If you already have a regular spare, don't make the mistake of never examining it for low air pressure, dry rot, a damaged valve, or other signs of trouble. A good technique, if you change all four tires and you have an old spare that may be questionable, is to take the best of the four old tires and have it mounted on the wheel for the spare.

Decades ago, my old pal John and I were out in Sharon's and my garage trying to change the tires on our Volkswagen Squareback (like a miniature station wagon). That was during the brief period in Illinois when studded snow tires could be used. My studded tires were slightly oversized and gave the VW what almost amounted to off-road capability in heavy snow. The trouble was, John and I – both of us good-sized guys in our late twenties – could not get the old tires off. The lugs had been put on with one of the compressed air-powered units that lock them in really tightly.

We finally gave up, drove over to a service station with a functioning repair shop – you can tell how long ago this was – and a guy with more muscles than either John or I just snapped the lugs free.

The point is, have the lugs on your wheels tightened manually, so that you can loosen them without putting yourself in traction. Having a spare tire but being unable to get the old tire off would be beyond embarrassing in a post-disaster scenario. Conventional jack handles that incorporate the socket for the wheel lugs are okay as weapons when needed, but a **cross-shaped four-way wrench** – not very good as a weapon at all – is the most convenient tool for changing a tire.

A **storage container** should be kept in the vehicle, all the belts, hoses and fluids and bulbs, etc., that you have acquired as emergency spare parts stored within it. These emergency spare parts should be inventoried and a schedule developed for checking their integrity. With items that can go bad – again, ask the mechanic for his or her suggestions – rotate them and replace as needed. Remember to have a **tire inflator** that can push air into your tires by running off the cigar lighter. Learn how to use this before you need to know how to use it in an emergency and, instead of putting air into a soft tire, you let more air out. Been there and done that – accidentally, on someone else's car.

Another good idea is to keep a couple of cans of **Fix-A-Flat** or some other pressurized tire inflator on hand. These products don't work well on all sorts of flats, but they're cheap insurance against minor punctures.

An additional item you might wish to include is a **stout tow chain**, as long as you can safely attach the chain to your vehicle. Not only can you use it to help someone else, but someone else can use it to help you.

Additionally, include a good pair of **heavy cloth work gloves** and you might wish to inventory a set of **coveralls**. Water-resistant ones would be good. Rarely do automotive emergencies occur under ideal weather conditions. Have some sort of hand cleaner available.

Purchase some of the **blue industrial paper towels**, too, for a wide range of uses with the vehicle – everything from checking your oil to wiping off mud obscuring your side mirrors.

If you have a four-wheel drive vehicle, learn how to properly and safely use it in four-wheel drive. Practice. You'll have some fun and, when the chips are down, you'll be better and more confident behind the wheel. We know a nearby general practitioner who would always take his massive four-wheel drive pickup truck out for a ride anytime there was an ice or snow storm. I guess his theory was that, as a medical doctor, he might be called out to the hospital during dangerous weather and the smartest thing to do was to get used to driving in it. I am not recommending that you do that, but it worked for him.

Vehicles on slippery pavement demand caution. Vehicles that plunge into the

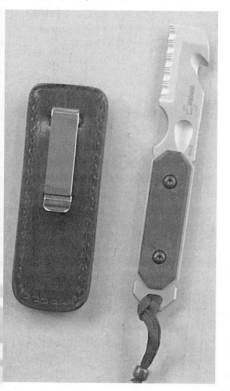

water demand instant action. Much of the lore of surviving a crash into the water involves windows. If you do anything with windows, it's got to be fast, before outside pressure from the water builds to the point that you cannot get the windows down. Power windows – in fresh water – will work for a time, but that won't do you any good if there's too much water pressure against the window. As soon as you hit the water, don't wait because you don't have anything to lose by trying. Try your power or crank windows right away. As close to simultaneously as possible, try opening the driver's side door, before the vehicle submerges more and the pressure precludes you opening the door.

This unit from Boker Plus is designed for cutting seatbelt webbing and, in general, to aid in vehicle extraction. A tool like this is something everyone should keep in the car.

Before the car is too submerged, start pushing on that door and keep pushing on it, especially if you couldn't get a window down. But, don't bet on that working. Sharon and I keep at least one **automotive glass breaker** in the car at all times. My **SureFire pen with its own automotive glass breaker** is very often with us, too, in the sleeve pocket of one of my **Woolrich Elite Series Tactical Algerian Field Jackets**. This or some other device actually made for smashing through tempered glass – there are automatic models and special hammers – will break the driver's window glass. With pressure only starting to equalize, you very likely will not be able to open the door. You'll have to crawl out through the opening, so make certain to clear enough glass so you can do this without slashing yourself. Either that or wait. On the plus side, tempered glass basically just breaks into little bits. The possibility of having to crawl through a window opening is also a good incentive not to gain too much weight, lest you find yourself too big to get through the window opening. In the worst case scenario, conserve your energy as the oxygen starts to run out, then hold your breath as the vehicle completely fills with water. Pressure will finally be equalized and you should be able to open the door a little bit at a time and swim to safety or clamber to the roof of the car and look for help, assuming the roof is

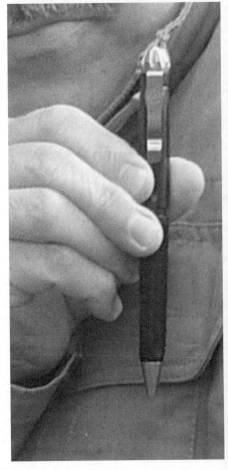

(above) Ahern carries a SureFire pen with an automotive glass breaker cap in the sleeve pocket of his Woolrich Elite Series Tactical Algerian Field Jacket. **(right)** Close up of the SureFire pen, with its automotive glass breaker cap.

only a foot or a few feet under the surface.

Now that you've looked to the care and feeding of a vehicle, and you have ascertained which fantasy vehicle, in an ideal world, would be perfect for your needs, and you know how to escape your vehicle, it's time to think about the stuff you want to always keep packed in the car's trunk or truck's tool box, etc.

Our son kids us that we keep so much stuff in the trunk of our car we have no room for groceries or luggage or anything "normal." To a degree, he's right, but I would rather be prepared for emergencies and have to be a little skillful at packing than have plenty of room and be caught unprepared. One thing we always keep in the trunk is a six-liter **Maspion Plastics water "can."** We change the water periodically. The container has a handle and a shoulder strap and seals tightly. We also carry a ventless one gallon four ounce plastic gas can, empty unless we are going seriously far afield. We have **lightweight sleeping bags**, **binoculars** and a Glock **trench shovel** along with some medical supplies. Don't forget the **flashlight**. For practical purposes, sometimes the **Henry Repeating Arms U.S. Survival Rifle** is stowed in the car, but I don't leave a firearm in any vehicle overnight. We also have an ice scraper for the windows, blankets, a shoulder bag for carrying incidentals, rope, etc.

Some of the items in Ahern's trunk, including a trauma kit, a fire extinguisher, a Henry Survival Rifle, an American Tomahawk Viet Nam Tomahawk, binoculars, emergency water supply, etc.

(top) The Henry U.S. Survival Rifle stows in its buttstock.
(above) Ahern cradling the Henry rifle. One of these belongs in every vehicle trunk.

Gerber Patriot fixed blade knife, ideal for keeping in the car.

Additionally, of course, we keep a number of other possible necessities to hand in the vehicle, to include a **stout fixed-blade knife**, a **multi-tool** – I like the multi-tools from both Leatherman and Gerber – and ordinary things like **dental floss**. There are **maps**, MapQuest routings to infrequently visited important places and there's a recent edition road atlas.

Of course, the personal kit belongs in the car when you're near the car or in the car and the **bug-out bag** (discussed in Chapter 20) belongs with you as well. If current events indicate there could be major events of the unpleasant kind on the horizon, there are things I would add, of course.

The www.ready.gov website advises you, as mentioned elsewhere in this book, never to let your vehicle's fuel load get below a half a tank. That is, perhaps, the most important bit of vehicle-related advice to be had. We have a relative – a great guy, really – who has two very dangerous habits. As much as we try to talk him into doing things differently, he refuses. The first of these two habits concerns gasoline. Granted, he drives quite a bit for business, but he

Some of the contents of the personal automotive kit.

lets the car's fuel gauge hit Empty and the low fuel light on his dashboard start blinking and he still keeps driving. Only when he's running on fumes does he stop for gasoline. I'm glad he's not an aircraft pilot!

His other dangerous habit is that he never carries very much actual money; sometimes, he carries no money at all. He doesn't even rely that much on an ATM, instead counting on pay-at-the-pump for his gasoline and using a debit card to pay for his occasional fast food lunch. He's quite physically fit and a very health conscious man, eschewing fast food rather than chewing it. But, for his continued good health in the event of a manmade or natural disaster, I would be profoundly grateful if this gentleman would carry money and never let his gas tank get below half. He won't take my advice, but you should. Remember, "it pays to plan ahead."

That vehicle you have could be your only means of re-uniting with your nuclear family in the event of an emergency. Or it could be your only possibility to flee to safety with your loved ones. Think of it that way and keep it as ready as the rest of your vital gear. When a crisis hits is not the time to get ready.

Other types of vehicles besides SUVs, trucks and cars can come into play as well. If you live near a large body of water or a river, it might prove handy to have a small boat or an inflatable available in the event that navigating that waterway or lake needs doing. And, in the event of flooding, row boats, inflatables, bass boats and the like can be used to help rescue people trapped by rising waters.

If you have a boat for fishing or other recreation, it could prove invaluable in some disaster situations.

In a disaster situation, don't even think about wasting gasoline on something as stupid as mowing the lawn. This excellent John Deere yard tractor can be used to haul gear with a small trailer and, if necessary, its tank can be drained so the gasoline can go into your transportation. In rear of photo, you will see a battery operated golf cart which is loaded with things to be hauled away.

Of considerable potential importance to the prepared community is the humble golf cart. Running on rechargeable batteries, golf carts are great for short-distance hauling of items which would otherwise be hand-carried or moved at the cost of some gasoline or diesel fuel.

Depending on where you are and when a disaster related situation arises, other vehicles – even something like a snowmobile or bicycle – might prove useful. Exercise all your options.

Transportation can be anything, and a bicycle that is well maintained uses no fuel. If you don't need a bicycle for transportation, it can become a component of an electrical generating system.

CHAPTER 16:
TO EVACUATE OR NOT?

Evacuation raises an ugly specter, of course, in which one renders oneself wholly dependent on the skill, intent and abilities of others. If you evacuate to a government-run shelter and you are armed, your arms will be confiscated (at least for the duration), this including not only firearms but sheath knives, pocket knives, a Leatherman tool or anything with a sharp edge or that can be used as a blunt instrument. You must weigh such situations carefully.

During extended civil emergencies, some misguided persons of authority might, indeed, dispatch police or other units to "collect" firearms in order to safeguard the populace. Under such circumstances, the prepared individual must let conscience and good judgment be his or her guide, the needs for the preservation of the nuclear family or extended family being the ultimate consideration and taking precedence over all other demands.

Of all the chapters in this book, the subject of this one has given me the greatest cause for introspection.

I recall hearing the horror stories of evacuees crowded into government-run refuge centers in the aftermath of Hurricane Katrina. Now, Sharon and I have never been what one might call "joiners." We sang in a church choir for a number of years some time back and I'm a member of the NRA. That pretty much describes the extent of our interaction with groups. We're not snobs. Maybe it's that since neither of us went to kindergarten, we never learned how to play well with others. I don't know. But surrendering our sovereignty and taking orders from people, however well-intended, doesn't sit well with either of us.

That said – and this is merely personal observation and not offered as advice – if a situation dictated evacuation, Sharon and I certainly would evacuate. We're not suicidal.

However, we would elect to be on our own, as a nuclear family, or link up with our extended family. Some prepared communities might elect to evacuate as a group, although the logistics would certainly prove challenging. We would not go to a refuge center and surrender self-governance, no matter how well-intentioned our would-be guardians might be. It's too dangerous.

The federal government's www.ready.gov website advises wisely that one should learn in advance of a crisis which emergency shelters would be open to pets; some are and some aren't. Dogs and cats are considered family members by many of us, and we wouldn't want to go to a shelter and leave family pets to fend for themselves. And, of course, there are some family members who may not be physically able to be evacuated without specialized assistance or equipment which might not be available during a crisis. What are you going to do with a 90-year-old parent who needs a walker and gets exhausted after just a few steps?

There are many questions which must be considered and evaluated before deciding on whether or not you would or could, under most conceivable circumstances, evacuate.

When Sharon and I wrote our well-known science fiction/adventure series, *The Survivalist*, we chose to set the retreat so carefully prepared by our char-

The Special Forces Medical Handbook is an ideal reference that can be taken with you, if you need to evacuate. It incorporates life-saving procedures well beyond the scope of normal First Aid if the situation calls for drastic measures.

acter "John Rourke" in the mountains of northeast Georgia. Obviously, one reason was that we ourselves lived (and still live) in northeast Georgia. But that was one of the least important reasons. Northeast Georgia is within easy driving distance of the Atlantic Ocean, but nowhere near enough to the coast to be subject to flooding as the result of a hurricane. We checked prevailing wind patterns and determined that winds affecting Rourke's Retreat would not usually have passed over a major city anywhere nearby, hence there would be time for airborne contaminants or nuclear fallout to dissipate before passing over Rourke's Retreat.

Mountains present strategic disadvantages to attackers and advantages to defenders. Northeast Georgia has fertile soil, four seasons (although summer does seem to last forever, at times) and a water supply ranging from adequate to abundant. Northeast Georgia is not in an identified flood plain. There is seismic activity, but it is minimal. I've never heard of an avalanche or mudslide in northeast Georgia and our "snow emergencies" are usually close to silly. There are no active or even dormant volcanoes nearby – that we know of. There is wild game aplenty for living off the land; and, if you are careful with crop selection, there are what amounts to three growing seasons. We have a number of navigable rivers.

Am I working for the Georgia Tourism Board? No. We chose where we were going to live – Sharon and I, as were our children, were all born in Chicago – and we chose where Rourke's Retreat would be based on perceived geographic and climatic advantages. Now, we could do that because of our occupation as writers. Most people don't have that much flexibility. Where we live, there is extremely little likelihood we'd have to consider evacuation in a disaster emergency. We already live where evacuees from nearby larger cities such as Atlanta, Georgia, would evacuate to.

Consider where you live when determining your options concerning evacuation. Sharon and I spent three very pleasant days a few years back staying in a rented condominium literally right off the ocean in St. Augustine, Florida. The beach was beautiful, as was the ocean itself. If a hurricane were on the way, however, it would be foolish not to consider evacuating a structure built on low-lying land about 200 yards from the surf's edge – probably less than that during periods of higher tides.

Where you live should figure heavily into your plans for what to do during a disaster. If you live in a major city, terrorist action is more likely to directly affect you than if you lived in a town of 3000 people. If you live on the northern Great Plains, blizzard conditions are a far more likely threat to you than to those of us living in northeast Georgia. Conversely, you will likely be vastly better prepared for a snow emergency – in terms of clothing, gear, and experience – than people living in the usually sunny South. An inch or so of snow went all but unnoticed when we lived in Chicago. In Georgia, an inch of snow is a life-altering event and, in preparation for this terrific "snow storm," there's such a run on milk and bread at the supermarkets that the shelves are nearly picked clean. Sharon calls it a "nesting instinct," to prepare for the situation by making certain to have these items for one's family – even if you had just purchased milk and bread the previous day.

Assess your situation and evaluate how location will impact your choices and integrate these factors as you formulate your plans.

If you will have to evacuate or merely travel some considerable distance to link up with the nuclear family or the extended family, you'll want more than the basic necessities of the individual kit. You'll want something on a larger scale, what some call a **"boogie bag"** or **"bug-out bag"** (For more information on the bug-out bag, see Chapter 20).

The concept of the boogie bag is simple. Assume the pizza has hit the proverbial fan and things are splattering everywhere around you. There's no time for anything but to hit the trail fast. Everything you need for doing that – theoretically – should be in your boogie bag, an advanced form of the individual kit that is intended for longer term use. You grab it and drive or run or whatever toward safety or toward reunion with your nuclear family or extended family.

The bug-out bag would likely be kept in your car, too large to be hauled in and out of the work place on a daily basis. When you're home, the car is in the garage or in the driveway. Let's say you take your wife to the movies to see the next John Voight flick and you discover you're in the throes of a disaster by the time you exit the theater. Your boogie bag is with you. You might use it to evacuate, or you might use it to just get home and stay there. In the final analysis, it's the choice of you and your loved ones – and no one else's.

If there is mandatory evacuation by force, you may find yourself faced with some tough choices there, too. Always remember, the welfare of the nuclear family and the extended family is the ultimate concern. As John Wayne memorably said, "A man's gotta do what a man's gotta do." The same applies for women, of course.

CHAPTER 17:
SAVING MEMORIES

Memories of loved ones can be attached to things like photographs. This photo shows Sharon's parents on their wedding day on top, a certificate on their twenty-fifth wedding anniversary and, at bottom, when they celebrated their fiftieth.

Because of who and what we are – human beings – there are things we care about because of their association with people or places or times which we hold dear, keep in a special place in our hearts and minds. Some certain items are irreplaceable and their loss leaves an empty space in our lives. A photo, or perhaps something else – whatever the item may be, we need to guard against loss.

Whether through flames, rising waters, high winds or terrorist atrocities, photos of loved ones, treasured records of a family written in a Bible or elsewhere, bride and groom figures from atop a wedding cake, great grandpa's hunter case watch, or any number of other items of personal value, once lost, are gone forever. That is, unless you plan ahead.

Quite a number of years ago, the house belonging to a friend of ours burned to the ground. No one was hurt in the conflagration. Sharon and I knew that the man and his wife truly doted on their then-little boy and had a comparatively large number of photos of the young fellow. We assumed these were lost as a result of the fire. The man and his wife had, however, planned ahead. These were the days before digital cameras, of course, so photos always involved film of some sort. Even though the photos were lost, duplicate prints and – importantly – the negatives were wisely stored in a bank safety deposit box.

There are categories of memorabilia, namely 2) those items that are "one of a kind" and 2) those things that can be duplicated. The one of a kind items present a problem, one that is not insoluble, yet one demanding that choices

be made. Let's use the example of the hunter case watch passed down from great-grandpa. If you keep it at home in order to take it out and look at it from time to time, you should keep it in a **home safe**, one that has a good degree of fire resistance and can be bolted into concrete. For added protection, place the watch along with similar valuables – great grandma's engagement ring, etc. – inside a locked **fire-resistant box**.

If you can't afford the safe, try for the fireproof box and stash it someplace that would hopefully be hidden from a thief.

A surer solution, and one that is less expensive in the short term than purchasing a quality safe, is to rent a **safety deposit box** from a bank that you trust. A safety deposit box allows privacy for viewing of contents and will likely be more secure than

Important papers such as deeds and birth certificates should be safeguarded.

the most secure home safekeeping – better alarms, possible armed guards, etc. Typically, safety deposit boxes are housed within huge vaults, so a bad guy of any sort or wind or fire or flood will have to get through that sealed vault door in order to get to your double-locked box, which can also have still another lock attached to it, the key to which you keep in your possession.

If a home vault is your answer, make certain to get a good one. The locking system employed by **Champion Safe Company** is a noteworthy example. The combination dial is lockable with a key. Once the key is turned to free the dial, the dial must be brought to the precise series of number positions. This unlocks the vault door. Several large bolts are slipped free from the box surrounding the door as the safe handle – now free – is turned.

But look at this Champion Safe from an intruder's point of view. If he doesn't have the key or isn't good at lock picking, he might break the lock on the combination dial and jam the dial. If he doesn't have high-tech safecracking equipment of the kind used in spy movies, he'll be stuck trying to blow or drill

Family pictures can be copied onto disc or emailed for safety to a friend or even to yourself.

the box. Blowing a safe that's better than five feet tall and built to be fire- and burglar-resistant could be extremely hazardous and would require skills the average person doesn't have. Drill the box, then. Drill through the combination dial. But if the intruder drills anywhere through the door – perhaps to insert explosives – he'll shatter a glass panel within the door itself. When that happens, an extra lock comes into play, freezing the door so thoroughly shut a Champion technician will have to pay you a call and open the safe; you won't be able to.

The Champion Crown series safe typically weighs over 1500 pounds when empty, so it's unlikely anybody's going to try to carry it off without heavy equipment. Don't forget, it's bolted into concrete for good measure – assuming you've got concrete floors or installed a pad.

For important photographs and important documents, there's a simple, low cost alternative solution. Scan the photos and documents, unless they already exist electronically, and copy them to CD. Home movies of the kids that weren't made on DVD should be transferred to DVD. Most of us have friends or relatives who live in other parts of the country or even in other countries. Contact these friends and family members and ask them to do you a favor and keep a copy of the discs for you. Volunteer to do the same for them. If the entire country or the entire world goes into disaster mode, it would still be unlikely that the several copies of the discs would all be lost or destroyed. If the disaster is greater still, viewing the contents of the CDs or DVDs may become a moot point, at any event. Dead men not only tell no tales – they watch no discs!

In an instant emergency, when it will be impossible to ship discs, but there is a little time and the internet is still available to you, copy what you can and email these items to anyone. Once things get back to normal – which they likely will after a time – you'll be able to get into your email and go into the "Sent" file and retrieve your important attachments from wherever you wind up.

CHAPTER 18:
SPECIAL SITUATIONS, SPECIAL NEEDS

Try as we might to come up with blanket solutions for the adversities life throws at us, we can never generalize. We can only strive to be as informed as possible before making our decisions – especially those with potentially life-altering consequences, such as what might well be encountered in the aftermath of disaster. Decades ago, I wrote a monthly magazine column titled "Terrain and Situation." That's a military concept, of course, but it's a life concept, too. Your options depend on where you are and what you need to accomplish.

Whatever the reason, in the event of a disaster you'll probably be unlucky enough to be an immediate eyewitness to whole bunches of people acting stupid because of some freak of nature or the actions of a malicious person or group. Not to sound negative or anything, but large numbers of people, no matter how much they are exposed to life-saving information, won't even bother to listen and will never prepare.

Most people are pretty intelligent once you get past their preconceptions and prejudices, yet some people aren't. During emergencies, this mentally under-endowed minority – they arise from all races, every societal stratum, all educational backgrounds and both sexes – loses most or all sense of logic, and these folks might not have had a great deal of that to begin with. They do stupid things. Some of these things are mean-spirited. Some are self-destructive. All are potentially dangerous to your continued well-being and your mission in the aftermath of a disaster.

When things get bad, you just want to get home and re-unite with your nuclear family. Or you want to safely wait it out at home with your nuclear family or extended family of prepared community. They, on the other hand, are anything from sneaks to gangsters to predators to wild men.

You have real-world problems to consider. For example, the National Council on Disability (www.ncd.gov) has, as this is written in August of 2009, just released a report concerning the inability of disaster plans to meet the needs of America's 54 million people with some sort of disability. What if you are one of these people? What if you're in a wheelchair, or are blind and use a guide dog, or are partially deaf? What then?

What if a member of your nuclear family is cognitively challenged? How do you help that person to understand why part of the city is on fire, or why there are no lights, or why you have to leave your home and your possessions and the goldfish behind and drive along a highway you've perhaps never travelled before?

The facts indicate that most formalized disaster planning incorporates little consideration, at best, to those with special needs. That being the case, it is even more vital for the prepared individual who has a personal disability or has a disabled person or persons in his or her nuclear family or extended family to tailor emergency preparations to such special needs.

There are other special situations, of course, which require special treatment. Despite recent moves by various pharmacy chains to discount prescription costs by filling 90-day supplies instead of 30-day supplies, large numbers of people, for whatever reason, still only take a 30-day refill. This is poor plan-

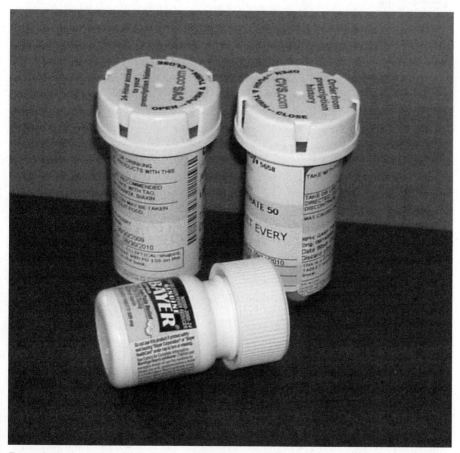

Prescription and over-the-counter medications should be kept in suitable quantities.

ning and should be avoided if practical financially and/or otherwise. Certainly, if you've just filled your 30-day supply of some vital medication, you've got three weeks or so for things to get back to some semblance of normalcy.

But what if you were going to pick up a fresh supply of heart medication or diabetes testing strips or insulin or some similar prescription on Wednesday and the manmade or natural disaster takes place on Tuesday and, by the time Wednesday arrives, obtaining anything from the pharmacy proves impossible? What do you do then? Clearly, you've got a problem.

Planning ahead must not only concern the broad strokes but the fine points as well. It'll do you no good at all if you are otherwise perfectly set to ride out the ice storm or the terrorist incident, but are gravely ill or worse.

What if you're a Girl Scout Troop Leader and you have 18 Brownie Girl Scouts you're taking on a field trip? What if you are a teacher and you have 20 or so fifth-graders to look out for in your home room class? What if disaster strikes then?

Obviously, many organizations, schools and businesses will have their own emergency plans worked out well in advance. As Robert Burns tells us often happens with "The best laid schemes o' Mice an' Men," however, things don't work out according to plan. As a prepared individual, you need to think such situations through well in advance of any actual incident so that, if the need arises, you'll have some idea of what to do in the first moments of the emergency and won't be caught without a clue. It is not at all far-fetched for us to consider that school, church, athletic and social groups and organizations should undertake to develop emergency planning at the most intimate levels. As discussed here, the United States government, through its various branches, encourages individual and group planning. There are even available, through some government agencies, downloadable activity books for kids.

Schools have fire drills so that teachers and children alike will know where to go and what to do in the event of the real thing. Procedures are established. The attendance roster is taken by the teacher or an aid and attendance is again taken once the class has reached its appointed waiting area. The names of those students present are matched against the names of everyone in attendance that day. With such a procedure, the teacher can immediately realize that little Johnny is missing and start to search for him.

But what if little Johnny *is* missing? What is the procedure to find little Johnny? Who goes back into the building, if anyone does? Who coordinates with the fire, rescue and police personnel who are the first responders concerning the missing little Johnny?

Decades ago, when I was a teacher, the first high school I taught at virtually abutted a prominent university with its fair share of leftist campus radicals and was neutral territory for two of the largest urban fighting gangs in the United States. We periodically had bomb scares and had to evacuate the building. Planning for the evacuation might have been excellent, but its execution was beyond stupid. Because of permissiveness, little was done beyond pleasant encouragement to get the really cool gang bangers out of the building. They deliberately walked as slowly as possible and lagged behind just to show they were unafraid. Once the building was exited, everyone stood around, maybe a dozen yards from the building itself. Had an actual explosion occurred, scores of kids – who would have suddenly ceased worrying about looking cool – would have suffered cuts and abrasions and possibly worse. Planning is great, but realistic planning is the only kind that's worth the time expended.

What do you do if you are away on vacation or on business and a manmade or natural disaster catches you away from your nuclear family, away from your personal kit – much of which you can't take on a plane except as shipped luggage – and away from any financial resources beyond what you have in your wallet or money clip? You don't know the area, you have no real contacts or personal resources there and the airplanes aren't flying – just as in the immediate aftermath of the September 11 attacks when President George W. Bush wisely ordered all non-military, governmental or emergency aviation grounded.

Honestly, I don't know what to tell you to do. If you are in the airport or some other reasonably secure location – and most major hotels might not be that secure – you should probably stay where you are and contact home and loved ones as rapidly as possible. Other options include renting a car and driving home, if that's practical and the roads are sufficiently clear and transportation is available. Obviously, if you live in Toledo, Ohio, and your business trip took you to Phoenix, Arizona, driving is likely not going to be as practical as you might wish.

You'll have to determine what your best guess is concerning the duration of the incident and then consider your alternatives. If it seems obvious that the manmade or natural disaster's effects will pass within a few days or a week or so, if you can survive safely where you are at, stay there. If you can honestly evaluate the situation and determine that there would seem to be no end clearly in sight for weeks or months or longer, then you have to determine whether you venture out.

Much of the decision-making involved will not be so totally predicated on what your situation is as what the condition of your nuclear family is. If you know that your nuclear family will be in desperate straits without you there – and, set your ego aside for a moment and be realistic – then this will obviously seriously color your decision-making process and your eventual choice of action.

When Sharon and I began our post-holocaust science fiction series *The Survivalist*, chronicling the adventures of character John Rourke in the immediate and long-term aftermath of a nuclear war, Rourke was on his way back home after a business trip. He lived well north of Atlanta in a semi-rural area of northeast Georgia. His plane was diverted from its pre-arranged landing in Atlanta and was ordered west. It eventually crash-landed and Rourke found himself in Arizona, with most of a continent between himself and his wife and children, about whom he had absolutely no information. When commercial aviation was stopped after the September 11th attacks, many persons found themselves similarly stranded and had to make tough choices.

There is no true way to plan ahead for such an eventuality. There are some things you can do, however. Train yourself to think analytically and clear-headedly so that you can accurately and concisely evaluate the facts of the situation into which you have been thrust. Learn to carefully consider and explore all possible likely options.

And, even in an age when you are severely limited as to what you can bring aboard an aircraft, no one can stop you from wearing or having with you a good, comfortable, sturdy pair of cross trainers or hiking boots, a couple of pairs of athletic or boot socks and a map of the city you'll be visiting and a map showing the various routes between that city and where you live. If you try taking a compass aboard on your person, the Homeland Security people may think you're acting strangely. **G.I. Lensatic Compasses** and similar precision instruments aren't exactly cheap, but an inexpensive compass and some of the other items of your personal kit can be brought along in shipped luggage. You may be able to buy a knife and some other necessities in the city you're visiting. If you can't, and you've thought things through creatively, you'll soon discover a "field expedient" that will serve until something better comes along. Man or woman, no one can stop you from wearing or packing a sturdy leather belt with a heavy brass or steel buckle through which the belt can be wound several times in order to make a flail you can use as a weapon, failing all else.

Whatever the special situation in which you find yourself, keep your head, consider the options and then do what logic best suggests.

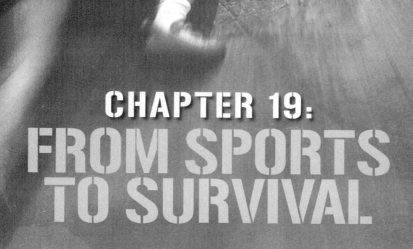

CHAPTER 19:
FROM SPORTS TO SURVIVAL

In 1457, King James II of Scotland banned playing golf, which had already been around, apparently, for hundreds of years. The ban was largely ignored. James III banned it again. Same results. As golf increased in popularity, however, there seemed to be a directly attributable decline in Scottish prowess on the battlefield. It seems that the ability to hit a birdie was becoming more important than the ability to hit a baddie in battle with an accurately-launched arrow. This is not an apocryphal story.

Today, of course, archery is still practiced, both competitively for sport and for hunting various game animals. A fine archer with strong nerve can still make a good account of himself/herself in the anti-personnel context, as needed.

There is, throughout history, a direct relationship between martial activities and sport, sport often modified directly from battle skills. Fencing is an obvious example. Warriors fought with swords in the Bronze Age, of course, as early as the 17th century B.C. Schools teaching swordfighting skills date to at least the 12th century A.D. in Europe, with one of the earliest surviving texts dealing with use of sword and buckler (a small shield) written in Latin and High German. Classical fencing, as seen today, is rooted in the 16th century "schools of defense," in which European gentlemen learned how to handle a rapier or small sword for defense of their honor on the street.

Discounting sports such as beach volleyball, synchronized swimming and ice dancing, we also have Olympic sports such as the marathon. This is based on the story of Pheidippides, a heroic runner who, in 490 BC, raced from Marathon to Athens to deliver battlefield intelligence concerning the defeat of the Persians, giving over his happy intel before dying as a result of his effort.

Horseback riding events in sport are largely derived from military necessity. A perfect example can be seen in George S. Patton. He participated in the 1912 Summer Olympics, the fifth modern Olympiad and the first modern era Pentathlon, which incorporated riding. A 1909 graduate of the United States Military Academy at West Point, Patton studied horsemanship and saber. He distinguished himself in most of the Pentathlon events, finally finishing in fifth place. In the pistol shooting event, Patton used a .38 caliber revolver, rather than a .22, actually sticking to what was then a common military caliber. Patton became the United States Army's youngest "Master of the Sword," designed the Model 1913 Cavalry Saber, and developed a training technique for the mounted use of the saber.

The list of martial-related sports goes on. Just consider boxing and wrestling. Both discus and javelin, each an element of the ancient pentathlon, have

The martial saber such as this Windlass Steelcrafts replica of a Colonial American saber has given way to certain of the fencing competitions of today.

(right) These modern versions of swept hilt rapiers remind us of the Schools of Defense from centuries gone which led to the sport of fencing.

(bottom) A Katana at top and a Wakazashi below – edged weapons such as these led to the practice of Kenjitsu and other types of oriental fighting techniques turned to sport. These are from CAS-Hanwei.

combative origins, as do Wrestling, Long Jump and Foot Racing. The modern pentathlon includes cross-country steeplechase, cross-country running, swimming, epee fencing and pistol shooting.

Biathlon, which incorporates accurate rifle shooting and cross-country skiing, has martial origins. Numerous sports can trace their origins to battle. Games ranging from chess to football all have connections to martial activity, whether strategy alone or in conjunction with violent action. Although firearms are used in all manner of peaceful endeavors today – such as wheelchair-bound persons competing in precision handgun target shooting – their origins are distinctly martial.

In a disaster-related survival situation, there is no direct connection to golf, curling, basketball, soccer, bowling, tennis and the like. Yet, they are marvelous sports and healthy pastimes. They build endurance and stamina, strength and co-ordination and help one to accurately judge distances and angles and vectors. There are other equally fine sports, the practice of which can aid directly in the acquisition of useful survival skills and afford one tools which can be used in survival and defensive situations.

The obvious first choice is the hunting of small and medium game with rifle or handgun or bow. Shotgunning sports will enable you to bring down a bird on the wing. These all translate into the acquisition of food. Stalking skills employed in certain styles of hunting will translate to tracking and silent/unobtrusive movement which might be required in certain disaster-related survival contexts. Tracking skills for locating game are directly relevant to such scenarios.

Camping in the deep woods or building a snow cave above the tree

line, rock climbing or rappelling, hiking or orienteering – all involve outdoor skills which teach everything from self-reliance and confidence to how to live off the land.

The black powder sports not only afford one the opportunity to practice primitive shooting skills, but such long term survival skills as brain tanning hides and making footgear can be learned. The knife or tomahawk you learn to throw for sport can be a trusted implement in a survival situation resulting from a disaster, manmade or natural.

We hear a great deal about childhood and adult obesity in the United States and how so many persons – young and old alike – clog their arteries and pile on useless calories while their greatest exercise is bench-pressing the remote or curling a bottle of beer or a bag of chips. Healthy outdoor activity – whether it's as simple as hiking or as demanding as an Iron Man competition – can help to prepare you for situations which might likely be encountered in the event of natural or manmade disasters. A fine example is individual or competitive cycling. Cycling is an endurance sport of the highest order, building muscle and providing superior cardio training. When the bicycle is a mountain bike, the sport incorporates different challenges and could even include orienteering.

But not all preparation needs to take place in the outdoors. Regular regimens of body building with free weights or machines and physical training through calisthenics or the use of treadmills and stair climbers builds strength and endurance. Every extra pound you carry – and most of us carry extra pounds – will help to tire you out and represents some vital piece of equipment or foodstuff or water you might have to leave behind. Building up muscle only takes regular, effective activity. The nature of the human body takes care of the rest. The late Charles Atlas was, in fact, the equivalent of the "98-pound weakling" as a young man, but through training and perseverance he became a model for young men everywhere who wanted to have a better body. Following his program delivered the results. Today, his program goes on, and young people also have celebrities such as Arnold Schwarzenegger and Lou Ferrigno to inspire them in strength and fitness training.

Hunting and fishing can afford you the opportunity of eating healthier foods. Venison, for example, has considerably less fat in it than meat taken from domestic cattle. Fish is a natural source of proteins and healthy oils – and I should eat more of it. Regular vigorous exercise – of course only entered into after consultation with a physician – will make you better able to enjoy the skills you already practice and those skills you might need to or only wish to learn.

Play golf, but leave the cart at the club house. Try walking instead. And don't forget to practice your archery!

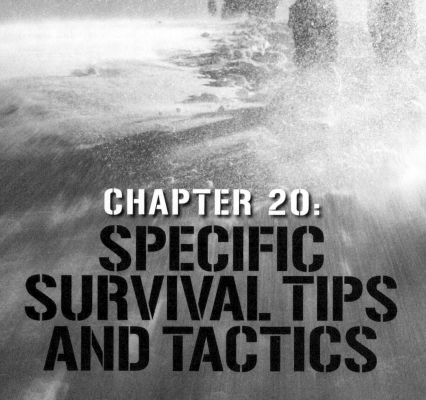

CHAPTER 20:
SPECIFIC SURVIVAL TIPS AND TACTICS

Surviving Winter Storms and Blizzards

Blizzards and snowstorms are among the most common disruptive events in north America. Since more than half of the United States can be expected to experience heavy snowfall at least periodically, let's take a moment and review basic winter survival skills.

If you live in an area where the possibility of blizzard – one of the most dangerous weather-related phenomena – is very real, the only sensible thing is to be equipped to withstand the cold, the heavy volume of snow, the high winds and the white-out conditions. The greatest dangers arise not when one is safe at home – although there may very well be issues with which to contend and high-volume snow can severely strain the integrity of some structures.

The worst case scenarios involve being caught out in a blizzard.

If you live in blizzard country, you need to keep a specialized extreme weather survival kit in your car at all times. To do otherwise is flirting with death. Obviously, you'll want a conventional **First Aid kit**. But, beyond that, you need to address warmth, nutrition, and the ability to summon help and wait for it to arrive. During whiteout conditions, or even just very heavily falling snow, it is even easier than usual on slippery surfaces to accidentally drive off the road. When blizzard conditions strike, you should pull off the road, at any event.

Regardless of how it occurs, you may become stranded in your automobile. You are better off by the side of the road or off the road in the shelter of your vehicle than you would be trying to walk out, whether following the road or, worse, cross-country. If you're stranded in a blizzard, as quickly as you can, after determining the condition of everyone with you in the car, you must try to get some sort of pennant up so your car may be more easily spotted. This used to be easier in the days of external antennas. Hanging it out a window will have to do. FEMA recommends that the flag be fluorescent, all the more easy to be spotted. You must make certain that your exhaust pipe is clear of snow or debris which could clog it. Be careful, because the pipe will likely be hot. Be ready to re-examine the exhaust pipe at regular intervals.

Things to do while outside of the car should also include carefully surveying your surroundings. If you see an actual structure – the proverbial farmhouse – where it seems likely you can find better shelter than your automobile, try to carefully gauge distance and snow depth. If you are quite confident you and any other members of your party can make it, try for it. Remember to shut off your car, in the event you have misjudged the situation and must return to the vehicle.

Immediately, try your **cellular telephone** and/or your **satellite phone** and/or your **CB radio**. Cellular phones most likely will not work far from civilization. Satellite phones are too expensive for most people to own. CB radios aren't as commonly encountered as they once were because of the proliferation of cellular telephones and have limited range. Assuming you cannot immediately summon help, you've got to be ready for the long haul. Hopefully you informed a family member or friend or colleague where you were going and you stuck to main roads, avoiding little traveled "short cuts" and side roads. That way if you don't arrive at your destination, you'll eventually be missed.

Open your trunk and get out your extreme weather gear. You should have blankets in sufficient quantity that the maximum number of persons in the vehicle would be accommodated. The **lightweight survival blankets** or just old blankets – not the threadbare kind, of course – will help all in the car to retain bodily warmth. And, cast bashfulness aside; share body heat under the blankets. FEMA recommends exercising to keep up circulation and body heat and using available materials, such as seat covers and floor mats, for added insulation.

You'll have a **shovel** of some sort. Snow shovels will usually be at the home or office. I'm talking about something the size of a trench shovel. I like the Glock one. This will aid you in keeping the windows free of drifted snow so that one or more windows downwind of the storm can be opened as needed. Make certain the window does not allow tailpipe emissions to enter the car. I would go with a window open at least a crack as much as possible.

When you are running the engine to get additional heat in the car – something to do for 10 minutes every hour, according to FEMA – the window must be open a good crack. You want the free exchange of oxygen in and carbon dioxide out and you don't want carbon monoxide byproducts from the car's motor to asphyxiate you. Make certain to turn off lights and all extraneous electrical equipment in the vehicle – except for hazard lights – in order to keep your battery strong. At night, run a dome light so that rescuers will see that your vehicle is occupied and not just abandoned. Many modern cars have multiple dome lights and you can choose to run only one, thus saving on battery depletion and bulb consumption.

Keep **high-energy, easily-stored food** as part of your extreme weather emergency kit; again, enough to keep the maximum number of occupants going for perhaps as long as 72 hours. Have appropriate containers partially filled with **water** (only partially filled to accommodate the contents freezing and expanding). If you're snowbound, get these into the vehicle at once and do what you can to melt the ice to where it can gradually be consumed. Dehydration is a serious risk under severe winter conditions.

A suggestion from FEMA that makes excellent sense is to use your feet to carve out "SOS" or "HELP" in the snow, highlighting the letters with rocks or branches. Your trench shovel can come in handy, here, too. In truly severe conditions, reconnaissance and rescue aircraft will be airborne as soon as it's safe, looking for people stranded like you are.

Keep your head. For example, if someone in the car must relieve himself or herself, don't let the person walk off out of a misguided sense of modesty and become lost. Use common sense.

Additional recommendations from FEMA include a **windshield scraper** and small **broom**. You should have a **battery-powered radio** – better yet, a dynamo crank style – with you in your bug-out bag gear (to be discussed). You should also have a **flashlight** in your bug-out gear. Extra **batteries**, rotated regularly, are an obvious inclusion. As far as conventional flashlight batteries are concerned – and I have no stock in the company – the Dura Cell batteries seem to be the longest lasting. FEMA recommends matches. Have a **disposable lighter** – Bics are great. FEMA advises having **spare hats, socks and mittens** in sufficient quantity for the anticipated maximum number of occupants. FEMA recommends a **tow chain or rope**, along with **road (rock) salt and sand, jumper cables and flares**. The car, of course, should have been safety checked and winterized.

Sharon was recently reading something that makes excellent sense, and it's also recommended by FEMA. Cover your mouth, as much as possible, and breathe through your nose. Limit talking, since this involves mouth breathing. Air inhaled through your nose will be warmed. Air inhaled through your mouth can dehydrate you. A face mask, a ski mask or something as simple as a scarf or bandanna can be used to cover the mouth.

If you are hiking, hunting, or exploring and blizzard conditions catch you off-guard, you will be in for some serious times. You must find shelter as quickly as possible or make shelter just as quickly. Hopefully, you'll have food and water and warm clothing and other necessities. Wise and experienced woodsmen will agree that you should never venture forth assuming that you'll only be gone for a few hours and, because of that, failing to have the basics with you.

Snow caves can be built. If you feel this might be necessary for your survival, read up on them and try making one in company with some friends under less than extreme conditions. You don't want to learn survival by the seat of the pants, although, many times, that is the way survival technique is learned.

Whatever you do, you need to seek shelter out of the wind. Tree boughs can help. Get a fire going as quickly as possible. You should have the basics for starting a fire with you. A **magnesium stick and some dry tinder** should be standard equipment when venturing away from civilization. Shavings whittled with your knife from the magnesium stick, along with the dry tinder, will get your fire started when you add the spark.

Try to keep from over-exertion and try to stay dry. Under severe cold temperatures, one's own perspiration immediately starts chilling the body and can be a serious hazard. If you are wet, get out of your wet things, as best you can, and change to dry clothes, if available. Try to dry the wet things with the fire you carefully built. Immediately, if you do not have a water supply with you, start melting snow. Remember the risk of dehydration. People naively think that you can just eat a handful of snow to prevent dehydration. It doesn't work that way. All it will do is serve to lower your core temperature.

Become sufficiently familiar with native vegetation that you can identify which trees have a bark that can be boiled down into a tea. For example, if you find yourself stranded near willow trees, the bark turned into a tea will work like Tylenol.

If you are at home and you have plenty of time to prepare, all systems – electrical, heating, plumbing, etc. – should obviously be checked in advance of the season. Flat sections of roofs need to be inspected for their structural integrity. Even peaked roofs can suffer an overload.

Always keep fuels for alternative heating systems readily available, but not so nearby as to create a fire hazard. Keep **fire extinguishers** handy in the event of an emergency. Fire extinguishers do no good at all if someone who might need to operate one doesn't know how. These extinguishers should be checked for adequate pressure. If kerosene heaters figure in to your emergency heating plans, remember that people die every year from fumes inhaled in poorly or unventilated enclosures.

In winter weather conditions, we expend more calories. Regular nutrition is important. Alcohol consumption should be kept to a minimum because alcohol makes one feel warn when one is not warm. We've all heard stories of drunks found frozen stiff in an alley, with their coats open or even removed. A belt taken from the friendly St. Bernard rescue dog's keg may help to bring you back. Drink the entire little keg and the opposite effect is more likely.

And remember those most insidious of cold-related dangers – frostbite, hypothermia and overexhaustion. Frostbite attacks the extremities first, and can cause the loss of toes, fingers, earlobes and the tips of noses. If you get your extremities too cold or too cold and wet, frostbite will strike. At the least, you'll feel the cold more the next time. At the worst, affected portions of the body will start to turn black and die, then have to be removed. Ears, toes, fingers, nose tips and the like are the potential casualties here. It's not being macho to go without gloves – mittens will keep your hands warmer still – or keep your ears uncovered. It's just being dumb!

Hypothermia can assault your kidneys, liver and other organs – or it can just kill you. The human body is more resilient than many of us think, but is designed to function properly within a certain range of temperatures and, when that range is exceeded in either direction, the human body can fail. Obviously, children, old people and domestic animals need to be looked to when such terribly low temperature ranges come into play, especially in conjunction with high wind conditions.

Overexhaustion of the type caused by shoveling heavy, wet snow can overtax an already strained heart, which is pumping more rapidly than normal just to keep the body warm. Walking through high snow drifts is quite labor intensive. During the snow storm which crippled Chicago in 1967, I had the necessity of trudging several miles through snowdrifts almost up to hip level. It was quite an experience, and one that I'll never forget and don't wish to repeat.

When merely covering up or adding layers of clothing is not enough to promote and sustain adequate bodily warmth, **battery-powered electri-**

fied clothing and other accessory wear exists to help warm you up. Battery operated socks, etc., can help to raise the temperature of one's feet and guard against frostbite. Frostbite can hit you before you are fully aware of it. With either frostbite or hypothermia, the body must be warmed slowly, in the case of frostbite to promote the return of circulation to the affected area. One must be careful, also, that when working under such low temperatures one does not perspire. The perspiration that forms on the body will chill the body even more and can well bring about catastrophic results for the individual. This is a problem for research personnel working at either pole. As persons just trying to cope with an unexpectedly bitter cold snap in a disaster scenario, we will not have the specialized equipment and clothing, yet we may have to combat similar temperatures, depending on where we live.

As modern human beings, we are vastly better suited to dealing with extreme cold than with extreme heat. As someone who is strongly averse to summer weather – I've heard all the cracks about why do I live in Georgia if I can't stand the heat – I often point out that, relatively speaking, there's no practical limit to how much you can put on in order to conserve or promote warmth; but, when you're down to shorts and sandals, there's really nothing else left that you can take off.

The weather in Chicago in January of 1977, when our daughter was born at a hospital situated on the shores of Lake Michigan, was bitterly cold. I heard a figure for the wind chill that day on the lakefront which I will not repeat here because it seems all but impossible. As I walked less than a city block's distance from the hospital door to my car in the open parking lot – I was picking up Sharon and our daughter to bring them home – my thighs stiffened, my body was shaking and exhaled moisture in my mustache had frozen to the point where I could have broken off hairs.

This is, of course, extreme. There is a new wind chill factoring system devised by the National Weather Service. Maybe, if that new wind chill factoring system had been in use then, I wouldn't have felt so cold; or, I might have felt colder. "Wind chill" and wind chill temperature – essentially the same thing – is analogous to the heat index referenced earlier. It is how you feel – not hot, but cold. For example, if you have a temperature of 30° Fahrenheit and a 30 mile per hour wind, the temperature on exposed skin feels like 15° F. If you have an ambient temperature of 12° F and the same 30 mile per hour wind, it feels like a temperature of -10° F. If you have an ambient temperature of -12° F and a wind of only 15 miles per hour, you're actually dealing with -35° F in terms of what it feels like on unprotected skin. This wind chill factor only has a bearing, in practical terms, on humans and animals. Wind chill does not affect your car, which is a very good thing, since, if it did, a lot of us would be walking in the wintertime.

Some extremes of temperature, of course, will affect vehicles and other machinery adversely. An acquaintance of some years ago – an Army officer – related that when he served in Alaska and had a Volkswagen with an air-cooled motor, the weather was so bitterly cold that he was forced, at times, to keep the motor running all the time that the vehicle was parked outside, lest he would be unable to start it. Cold weather does interesting things with vehicles, such as freezing the radiator contents that are not properly treated with antifreeze. One particularly annoying automotive problem under extremely low temperatures is that any moisture captured in the door locking mechanisms causes the locks to freeze. This would likely not be as much of a problem with modern locks as it was years ago. Automotive windows will also freeze shut. Exhalation will condense on the interior of a windshield and freeze.

Ice Storms

A full-blown ice storm can be a full-blown disaster. The weight of ice on tree limbs and power lines can bring them down. Downed lines are, of course, a fatality waiting to happen. Driving is slow and hazardous. Walking is dangerous. Climbing steps is risking an accident. Serious ice storms are something about which you can do precious little.

But there are some preparations which will make it a little easier for you. There are various styles of commercially available **ice creepers**. These attach to existing foot gear in a number of ways. But ice creepers can be improvised, too. The idea is to have something sharp on the bottom of your shoes, either at the heel alone or at the heel and further forward, nearer to the toe. The improvised kind – I've seen it recommended that a strap combined with ordinary tacks will work in a pinch – would likely be best going just in front of the instep.

The idea with walking on ice is to do it as little as possible and be careful with foot placement for each step. If there is snow and there is ice, walk in the snow until you absolutely have to step on the ice. Sand spread on the ice and even ashes from a wood or coal heater will give you a little traction. Strew either in your path as you advance along the ice. Rock salt – like you would use for making ice cream – will give you some traction and will melt the ice under the right conditions.

Adding weight from snow or ice to trees not only plays havoc with power lines, but it can cause a limb to snap and fall on you with sufficient force to cause serious injury or death. Larger icicles can fall on you and possibly stab, concuss, or kill you. The effect of ice storms lingers long after the ice is melted, tree limbs and downed power lines being the major concern.

In the aftermath of any sort of storm, ice or otherwise, never try resolving a power line and limb issue by yourself. Leave this work to the professionals. It is beyond dangerous to attempt to do it on your own. Never drive over downed power lines and never assume that a line is for telephone or cable or anything else. Assume it is a downed wire with an electrical charge that can kill or maim you.

Surviving Wildfires

Wildfires – whether brush, forest or grass-fueled – require evacuation. That's all there is to it. End of discussion.

If such a fire is headed your way, you must realize that even with the best fire fighting equipment, stopping it from consuming your home or your neighborhood or your sub-division might very well be completely impossible. If you stay, and the house is consumed, you may be consumed with it.

That said, there are things you can do to help yourself. Our **NOAA weather radio** is always plugged in and on. It automatically trips over to battery power during a power failure. When there is the potential for a fire, an alert is broadcast. The mechanical sounding male voice tells us that there's a "Fire Weather Watch" and may subsequently inform us of a "Red Flag Warning." High winds and dry conditions set up the scenario. Remember, all that is needed then is the spark.

If you live in an area prone to calamitous wildfires, you may find yourself doing the same thing my grandfather did in 1934 – hosing down the roof. But, there are other steps to take well before there's a Red Flag Warning. Keep your property and surrounding property clear of old and extraneous brush. Don't have too many trees too close to the house. Have hose connections located on all sides of your home. Have adequate numbers of hoses in adequate lengths available and make certain that dry rot or sun damage hasn't rendered the hosing un-useable. Nozzles should be put on all hoses, thus allowing you to accurately target flames.

Keep in mind that, in the event of a fire, depending on your water source, there may be a serious drop in water pressure. Have sturdy, fireproof ladders available to facilitate watering roofs as needed.

If a wildfire is underway, you must listen to information sources and, if the fire is approaching but it is not yet necessary to evacuate, start getting the car packed right away. Prioritize what can be taken along in the car long before the actual event. For any sort of emergency which could possibly necessitate evacuation, have a pre-determined list of what you will be able to take and know exactly where those items are located. It would not be a bad idea to conduct an evacuation drill. It is the only way to know for certain if your list is realistic or not.

The website www.ready.gov advises that you should try never to let your automobile's gas tank get below half full. Sharon and I used to have a wonderful old Chevy Suburban with a thirsty 454 cubic inch V-8 under the hood. With half a tank and an open road, we could have gotten about 150 miles. The trouble is, if you must ever evacuate, you'll likely be in gridlock and your half tank won't get you anywhere near as far as you might hope. Indeed, never get below half, if you can avoid it. And, remain alert to the potential for a problem arising. When that potential exists at a sufficiently high level, keep the tank topped off. If it can be stored safely, you may wish to keep several gallons of fuel available in proper containers when a threat exists.

Remember, wildfires jump and shift direction and they come fast. Don't wait to lay those plans which might save lives and property.

Surviving Civil Unrest

It is good to trust your fellow man. Trust some of your fellow men, however, to be conscienceless. At various places in this work, I allude to the potential for persons who failed to prepare for the aftermath of a disaster trying to take what you have. That's a given. During the Cold War fallout shelter craze, there were good-hearted but soft-headed people who could not imagine how someone could seal himself in a shelter and refuse entrance to all the other men and women who wanted in. These same good-hearted people chose to ignore the fact that a shelter designed to accommodate six people, let's say, would be a death trap for 16 people. Was it better for all 16 to die, or was it better for six to live? Many good-hearted people were sickened by the concept of keeping firearms in a fallout shelter for defense against those who failed to prepare and wanted in forcibly.

But I'm afraid that someone taking what you have put away in preparation for disaster is only one aspect of being wary. Just think of ordinary, everyday crime. It never stops. With law enforcement stressed to the breaking point and stuck in gridlock, a state of emergency is a potential paradise for those who live by preying on the weak. They can do their thing, but you can't call a cop. Even if you can get through on your cellular phone, the cops almost certainly won't be able to get to you in order to protect you.

Ordinary thieves aside, there are some people who truly enjoy doing bad things to other people. It boils down to the old line, "It's a jungle out there." You better believe it is. During a natural or manmade disaster and its aftermath, however long or short the duration, there will be some considerable numbers of people who will feel more free than they have in their entire lives, who can, at last, do whatever they wish without the restraints of law, order and society. If you look at a movie like *The Road Warrior* and think it's silly, don't. The haircuts and the crossbows are silly, sure. The conduct isn't.

Bad guys – and gals, of course – will band together to do their thing. If they didn't much care about hitting people over the head with a piece of steel pipe or shooting someone in the back before the disaster, when police could be summoned or might just be cruising by and catch them, when alarm systems and cellular phones worked and the lights in houses and apartments were on instead of off and there were street lights illuminating the night – well, they certainly won't start acting lawfully and feeling compassion for those affected by the crisis. Looting will be routine. Fires will be set. Anyone trying to stand in the perpetrators' way will be a target.

If you are trying to get home through all of this, it won't be easy. If you reside in a highly urbanized area, you may well want to consider, as part of your planning for the Nuclear Family and the Extended Family, working out an arrangement with friends or relatives who live further from the heart of a major city – hence, a possibly safer area. That arrangement should be to join these friends or relatives. Necessity might suggest a two-stage arrangement, wherein, given appropriate circumstances leading up to a possible disaster scenario, you transfer the children to this safer location. If only one parent works outside the home, maybe the other parent goes, too.

If you elect to take this option and, indeed, can – lots of people don't have friends or relatives who live outside the more highly urbanized areas – your planning must be specialized. Develop alternate routes from your home or office or factory or shop that will get you out of the densely populated areas of the city and to your destination. Travel these routes, learn them, and determine their potential for safety in a crisis situation.

If you live in an area where it is legal for you to own firearms and concealed carry permits can be had – most states, as this is written – you may want to consider keeping a **serious-caliber, high-capacity handgun** available to you. If police cannot help and you stumble into something, it may be your own one and only source of safety.

It is very easy to dismiss this idea until you have been in a situation where the world around you is suddenly radically changed. Sharon and I have been in such situations, both because of weather-related emergencies and because of civil unrest. You don't forget these episodes and they alter your perspective forever. I've been eating in restaurants where four or five cops sat in a booth grabbing a hot meal, all of them with handguns quite visible, one or two of them with .30 caliber M1 carbines beside them. We've seen a major city shut down to the point that not even police cars or taxicabs could move and guys were hustling milk for children off the back of a semi-trailer truck, charging the equivalent of over $30 a gallon in today's money. I've walked a couple of miles through a major city without seeing a single moving automobile or any sign of a person.

These experiences give one pause for reflection.

In the final analysis, when the usual, comfortable trappings of civilization are peeled away, there is no one to whom you can turn for safety except yourself or a loved one or a trusted friend. Self-reliance means reliance on oneself and not on others. Certainly, trust those whom you love and call friend, but don't assume that everyone else is just waiting to be your friend. Be open-minded, of course, but trust must be earned by the people with whom you interact. To do otherwise on your part, especially in a crisis situation, is not wise.

You have an obligation to your loved ones and true friends, as well as an obligation to yourself, to get through the crisis and come out on the other side of it, alive and well. Self-reliance is little taught these days because society stresses collective, co-operative action rather than individualism and personal initiative.

Life is not lived by collectives and committees, however, but rather by individuals, individuals who bond with others for whatever reason. Even the bad guys do that, bonding with one another out of a common desire to loot and plunder and hurt.

Keep telling yourself that you'll make it. Use your head and always watch your back. Do that, and you've got a solid chance.

Surviving Terrorist Bombings

A general rule concerning terrorist bombings is that terrorists wish to inflict the greatest number of casualties possible, while at the same time calling attention to whatever their cause is. The bomb as a weapon comes in many sizes and many guises, and even if a bomb is discovered before detonation, there's no reason to suppose it can be disarmed.

The Alfred P. Murrah Federal Building in Oklahoma City following its April 19, 1995, terrorist bombing. Photo courtesy FEMA News Photo.

One of my oldest and closest friends is one of the world's leading conventional explosives experts. He and I were discussing the use of a bomb in one of Sharon's and my novels. In the course of our conversation, we came around to the topic of sophisticated bomb makers and the potential for disarming or neutralizing the sort of bomb that might be set to detonate inside a building. He said something that was terribly sobering, something I've never forgotten. If the bad guy really knows his job and does it right, as the attempt is made to disarm the triggering device, that very action will cause a triggering device deeper within the bomb to activate. In other words, trying to disarm the bomb will detonate the bomb. If the bad guy has a serious level of professionalism, any attempt to disarm the bomb or do much of anything else with it will cause it to explode. It is not like it is in the movies, unfortunately.

The National Counterterrorism Center website (www.nctc.gov) features an interesting breakdown of bomb types and standoff distances so that you can avoid being a casualty. The types are extremely interesting. A pipe bomb, for example, would typically contain the equivalent of five pounds of TNT (trinitrotoluene). If you were standing in the open, in order to be safe from this, you would want to be at least 850 feet away. The site lists various sizes of bombs up to and including a semi trailer truck that could hold the equivalent of 30 tons of TNT and would require you, for safety purposes, to be almost a mile and a half away in the event of an explosion.

The improvised explosives that terrorists use so effectively in the Middle East and elsewhere are usually not just explosives. When you are detonating a device in the middle of a crowd and you wish to inflict as much damage as possible, you combine with your explosives items such as nails and scrap metal. The explosive force of the bomb will propel these pieces of metal at high speed and the projectiles will act like a bullet impact, only worse because of the nature of the projectile. A casualty in such a bombing situation could be all but shredded.

The explosive belts that homicide bombers use are designed to be detonated in a crowd. Special homicide bomber belts or vests are made for females in order to simulate the bulge of pregnancy. The cavity thus created to give the proper look can hold a great deal of explosives or extra projectiles that will enhance the effect when the bomb is detonated. Using bombs in terror is not a new phenomenon. Some early examples of terrorist bombings can be cited by looking at the work of the Fenian Brotherhood (Irish revolutionaries). In 1881, they attempted to blow up a military barracks. In 1884, they destroyed part of Scotland Yard. In 1885, they bombed the Tower of London and London Bridge. Meanwhile, a bombing in 1886 in Chicago, during a labor rally, precipitated the Hay Market riot. France, Spain, and Russia – all had bomb related terrorist incidents, and this is just in the 19th century. The event that sparked WWI, the assassination of Archduke Ferdinand in Sarajevo, began with a bomb attack.

The popularity of bombs stems from the fact that there is no real defense against them. Certainly, you can stop likely suspects and question them or even commence to search them. If the person with the bomb is willing to die – as is so often the case – he or she can likely detonate the device as a search begins. A gun in the hands of a dedicated madman can certainly inflict a number of casualties, but nothing in comparison to the volume and nature of casualties possible from a moderately well-constructed bomb.

If you are a victim in a bombing and you survive, there are certain things you need to know. As you've probably seen in movies, something terrorists love to do is plant a small bomb inside a building that will cause a modest amount of damage but force an evacuation of the building. If memory serves, this technique was used in the United States in the bombing of a building not long ago. Once the occupants have evacuated to "safety," a second larger bomb is detonated in order to inflict mass casualties.

As the infatuation with terror grows within certain population groups, the inevitability of terror proliferating is unavoidable. If there is a small bomb and you evacuate, be cautious that you're not setting yourself up to be killed by the larger bomb. If a small bomb goes off in your parking lot or you hear gunfire from your parking lot, you should be cautious that this is not an attempt to get you and other people in the building to come to the windows so you can be more easily shot or receive greater injury from flying glass when a larger bomb is detonated.

You should be wary of vehicles that are unattended. This is very difficult when you have large parking areas or crowded street parking, but a parked van or automobile or box truck could be loaded with explosives that can be detonated remotely with something as simple as a cell phone signal or a timer.

If you are a "walking wounded" victim of a building bombing or other type of terrorist bombing, you should be cautious concerning abandoned vehicles that may contain the big bomb. If you are not seriously injured you should endeavor to help those who are, but try to get some distance between you and the original bomb site.

Surviving Chemical and Biological Terrorism

During WWI, the horror of chemical warfare was first truly realized. Not only men but horses and dogs were fitted with gas masks to help protect them from the comparatively primitive chemical warfare arsenal of essentially a century ago.

If you are the sort of person who wishes to be prepared for the widest range of contingencies and you include having a conventional gas mask as part of this planning, it must be remembered that such a mask with a proper filter will indeed provide protection from things like tear gas. The more modern chemical agents, however, which can enter your body through your skin as well as via inhalation, cannot be protected against with an ordinary mask.

If the bad guys somehow or other elect to secure and use chemical agents, your conventional mask will not protect you. In the immediate aftermath of September 11th, there was great concern, as discussed elsewhere in this book, about the potential for cropduster planes and other small aircraft to disseminate chemical or even biological agents over our cities. Such a technique is not terribly practical. It is much more practical to use a biological agent rather than a chemical agent and to disseminate it in a far more insidious fashion.

We are told, as this is written, to guard against the transmission of H1N1 virus by such simple means as coughing and sneezing. The precautions that we are undertaking in order to stave off H1N1 are something we should seriously consider as a regular aspect of our nuclear family's program to help avoid falling victim to a terrorist attack.

Chemical weapons are much better used by our enemies in a confined area, not subject to the vagaries of wind and weather. But hostile chemical attacks are not the only thingwe need to be prepared for. In the normal course of events, without any evil intentions, there are hazardous chemical spills, vehicular accidents involving hazardous chemicals and industrial fires and explosions in which chemicals are a factor. Chlorine, which we are so familiar with in our swimming pools, can have horrific effects on the human body. Once afflicted, according to the National Counter Terrorism Center, the chlorine gas

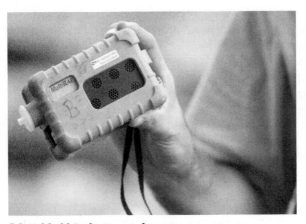

A hand-held toxic gas analyzer. Photo courtesy FEMA News Photo.

victim will be plagued for the rest of his or her life with an asthma-like condition. Chlorine gas that would be released as a result of an accident or as a deliberate act can seriously affect numbers of people, as the gas is carried on the wind.

Chemical and biological incidents are yet another reason to keep constantly informed concerning current events and to have a functioning emergency radio within earshot. In the event of a large-scale incident, you might be asked to evacuate. But there are some precautions you can take short of evacuation when certain types of toxic agents are present in the air. Let's say you're inside a typical house or apartment. Without running out of air, if you cannot evacuate or have not been informed that you should, you can take one room of your house and turn it into a safe room by combining plastic sheeting and duct tape to seal windows and doors and air vents. Don't forget to turn off the heating and air conditioning. This practice will provide you some protection under some circumstances for a limited time. Note: This is a short-term option, because eventually you will run out of oxygen. Sealing off an entire house this way will give you a larger oxygen supply but doing so is not a long-term solution. Neither is it practical.

Two of the most well-known agents for killing in large numbers are the biological agent known as anthrax and the chemical agent known as Sarin. In the immediate aftermath of September 11th, there were well-publicized anthrax attacks through the mail. Depending on the type of anthrax, the fatality rate can be horribly high. Cutaneous anthrax is the least lethal, with only 20 percent or so of untreated cases resulting in death. Intestinal anthrax can kill between 25 percent and 60 percent. The worst kind is inhalation anthrax, which is fatal in 90 percent of untreated cases and can be effectively treated only in the first few days of the infection.

Sarin is a manmade, colorless, tasteless, odorless liquid that can turn into a gas. It's an extremely effective chemical warfare nerve agent. You will recall the Sarin gas attacks that occurred in Japan in the mid 1990s. Sarin can get to you through the air, through direct contact or through contact with clothing that has been exposed to it. Symptoms evidence themselves anywhere from seconds to 18 hours after exposure.

Sarin mixes with water, so water can easily facilitate the spread of the agent. Since Sarin gas is heavier than air, in the event of a release, it will be found in lowlying areas. If you have been exposed to a modest form of Sarin in one of its forms, you must decontaminate as soon as possible, removing contaminated clothing, washing infected skin areas with plenty of soap and water and flushing with clear water. Remember that Sarin will stay on your clothing and you can re-infect yourself or someone who has touched your clothing can be infected. Mild contamination, if you act promptly and decisively, need not be fatal or leave any permanent disability. If you don't move quickly to help yourself and get help from qualified medical personal, Sarin can be fatal when it hits you with its host of nerve-related systems, which include everything from runny nose to excessive sweating to rapid breathing to diarrhea to confusion to blood pressure fluctuations. If you are hit by a substantial amount of Sarin, there is a substantial chance you will die.

Those of us who grew up on western movies and television shows understood the value of being able to "read sign." In the context of the Wild West, that meant tracking. For hunters then and now, it may mean looking for rub marks on tree trunks or animal stool. In case of a suspected chem or bio incident, the National Counter Terrorism Center has created a list of indicators. When you consider them, they're pretty obvious. For example, do you see dead birds or fish or animals? What about insects? Compare what you see to what is normal for the area. If normal conditions are absent, this could signal a chemical incident, either accidental or deliberate.

If you see a cloud just above the ground, for example, it could well be a poisonous gas or some other chemical. Stay away from it and get away from the area as quickly as possible. Contact 911 immediately and be alert for any changes you may experience. If you feel strange or sick, seek immediate medical assistance.

Surviving Influenza

I never thought I'd be that happy to be over 60. But, aside from still being alive and well, Sharon and I learned the other day that, if you were born before 1957, you have a better chance of not getting H1N1 because you would have been exposed to a similar flu strain. Even before learning such good news, we weren't as worried as we might have been, because we're not in the most threatened groups. Really young children and pregnant women, as well as teenagers and younger adults, are the most at risk, according to popular wisdom. This makes sense as far as younger children are concerned, because they are usually much more susceptible to respiratory illnesses. Similarly, persons with chronic conditions which can affect overall wellness are at risk. I had a heart attack some years ago, but I don't have heart disease. If I did, I'd be at greater risk. One of my relatives is diabetic. That heightens his risk, but he always gets flu shots and he's otherwise healthy. Taking the shots early on – once they are readily available – should prevent H1N1, we are told, or certainly reduce risk from the symptoms expressed. If you are an asthmatic – even the undiagnosed kind – you are at greater risk.

If you haven't had an H1N1 vaccination and you develop the classic flu-like symptoms – fever, diarrhea, nausea, trouble breathing, etc. – go to an emergency care facility or get together with your doctor. You'll likely be given an injection of Tamiflu or asked to use a Relenza inhaler. Either one is commonly said to lessen severity of the symptoms and get you back on your feet, but you must act quickly for best results.

The ultimate defense is to avoid crowds and wash your hands. H1N1 is a virus, which means it must enter your body either through your nasal passages or through your tear ducts.

Saliva will kill it if it tries to enter through your mouth. Until you can wash your hands or use hand sanitizer, don't rub your eyes or do anything you shouldn't with your nose.

When you wash your hands, sing. When Sharon and I were kids, we used to watch Richard Greene in the television series "The Adventures of Robin Hood." Part of the lyric from the theme song talked about Robin and his men always having the time to sing. Perhaps they were safeguarding against the Sherriff of Nottingham going after them with germ warfare? You should wash your hands with soap and warm water and continue washing long enough to sing "Happy Birthday" or something similar. The last few lines of "The Star-Spangled Banner" would work great, too. If you are religious, The Lord's Prayer is amply long enough to give you a good hand wash.

You do not catch swine flu from handling pork, but you should obviously wash your hands regularly. When infected persons cough and sneeze without covering their mouth and nose, they launch particles into the air. These particles can carry the virus right to you to inhale. Or, if someone coughs or sneezes into his hand, then touches something and you touch it right afterward, you can then get the virus on your hand and transfer it to your body by rubbing your eyes or doing whatever with your nose. When Sharon and I were dating, girls still wore gloves quite often when they dressed up. I can see the fashion coming back if H1N1 sticks around.

Door handles in public buildings and businesses can be a potential source of contagion. We all know about the handles on grocery store shopping carts as a way in which to pick up a virus. However, most supermarkets have available wipes which can be used to clean the part of the cart you contact most with your hands – or your child might touch while riding in the infant/toddler seat.

Our daughter always uses hand sanitizer after she tanks up her truck. How many people have touched the gas pump after coughing or sneezing into a hand? All you need is one person too many.

If you experience H1N1 symptoms, don't wait any longer than you have to. Get help. Once you are fully recovered from fever and other symptoms, give it another 24 hours before going back to your routine. Don't take risks.

Surviving Grid Failure

The modern world runs on electricity. In a blackout, the 21st century flows away like sand through your fingers if you don't eventually get the power back on. During the blackouts that sometimes hit major cities, elevators stop between floors, there are no traffic lights, no street lights. Consider the blackout of August 14, 2003, which eventually knocked out electricity to eight states and Canada's Province of Ontario. New York City and many other major cities in the northeastern tier were blacked out. This was especially scary since, in less than a month, it was to be the second anniversary of the September 11th terrorist attacks. It was a hot day, but not extraordinarily so. All that was needed was one system to start going down, putting an added load on another system in the grid. Overload that system and you have a ripple effect.

Various people address the issue of the North American electrical grids, but usually only after brownouts, rolling blackouts or something huge like the August 2003 event. It is generally conceded that the system needs upgrading. The more in need of repair the system, of course, the easier for a natural event – like a super heat wave or a serious ice storm – to strain the system beyond capacity. The more delicate the system, the easier it is for an act of sabotage to be successful against the system. In either event, the power goes out.

Without power, of course, the only electric lights are the battery-powered emergency ones such as those which come on automatically in theaters when the power goes out. All other lights – unless battery operated – cease to function.

In many emergencies, money will have to be substituted for ATM Cards and credit and debit cards.

Many commuter rail lines and all subway/elevated systems run on electricity. They stop and don't start again until the power is back on. Your car will run, as will buses, but neither will get very far because of the gridlock caused by non-functioning traffic lights. But let's say you do get out of gridlock. If you need gas, you're out of luck. The pumps run on electricity. If you don't carry much or any cash, or even if you do, you couldn't pay for the gasoline even if you could pump it because credit card machines and cash registers all run on electricity. So does the ATM machine.

If you work in a high-rise office building or live in a high rise apartment complex, the elevators will still be out, of course, and you'll have to walk up and down those steps, unless you are trapped inside an elevator. Elevators usually have escape hatches in the roof. If you can climb up and out, with help, you may be able to pry open the doors on the next floor above and clamber up and through.

The emergency lights in the stairwell won't burn forever, and you won't want to be in the stairwells when the lights finally flicker out. Air conditioning will be off, of course. If it's winter, even if you don't have electric heat, the blower is electrically powered, as is your thermostat, so you won't have any heat anyway.

If you are at home or make it there and have a fireplace, you can ward off the winter chill and burn wood or other safe-to-burn combustibles.

Better hope you have groceries, because the lights, the environmental system, the cash registers and the credit card machines – not to mention the laser devices that scan the bar codes – won't work. The store will be closed.

Some alarm systems will work; others will not. Most phones – land lines are little used these days – won't work, so you won't be able to call the police if you need them. Remember, too, that if looters are already out and about, experienced ones with a background in burglary will frequently cut telephone land lines in order to disable an alarm system. If you live in a gated community or have a gated driveway, your gate will remain in the position it was in when the power went out. We had friends, since deceased, who lived in the Hollywood Hills in a neighborhood surrounded by celebrities. Every time there was a power outage, they had to disconnect their gate so they could leave their house to take their little girl for a walk or get the car out of the driveway. If the power were still out when they returned, for security's sake – you guessed it – they had to reconnect the gate.

People will do things in the dark they'd never do in the light. And, the people who do really evil things in the light will be even more inclined to being nasty when the lights are out. Police and fire emergency response will be slower because of volume and traffic tie ups. Water is also pumped with the aid of electricity, so pressure will start to drop and the system will fail when the possible gas or diesel powered generators run down and are not serviced.

So much is computer-controlled these days that, since those computers not connected to an emergency power supply will not function, other systems and services will cease immediately or slowly, even if not directly dependent upon electricity. Airports will stop running. Even with emergency power for the tower, the flight boards and passenger screening systems would be down. Airports in major areas of the country and the world will all be affected because of flights which can neither get into or out of the area with the blackout. If it lasts long enough, more and more of the normalcy, upon which we so heavily rely and which we so often take for granted, will fail.

The larger the system failure, the more time-consuming it is to check the system so power can be restored. Overheated lines sag, of course, and can short out when automatic safety systems come into play. Drivers have more accidents under such unusual traffic and lighting conditions and there's greater likelihood of incidents exacerbating already difficult conditions and bringing more lines down when trees or utility poles are struck. The 2003 episode had power back surprisingly quickly, many areas restored later that evening or by early morning of the next day.

The electrical grid is an ideal target for terrorists. We know it and they know it.

Aside from acquiring **flashlights**, which usually require batteries or need to be re-charged, there are other things that can be done to provide you with light at night. **Solar-powered lights** are an ideal substitute. You leave the lights outside in the sunshine or in a window getting strong sunshine. On cloudy days, they'll take longer to charge, so you want more of the lights than you would normally use, the rationale being that you'll be able to keep lights in reserve. These lights can be found at lawn and garden supply stores and hardware stores. The light they emit is not as brilliant as conventional lighting, but they'll work when the regular lights won't.

If you have a **generator**, of course, depending on its size and your fuel supply, you can run some or your conventional electric lights. But fuel supplies may not be renewable and can dwindle quickly. A practical alternative is to find an **exercise bike** and build your own **power generating system**. You need a stationary bicycle – the exercise kind are already stationary – and an alternator and a 12-volt automobile battery. Search the internet and you'll find plans for how to construct the unit. The possibilities this technique presents are fascinating.

Elsewhere in this book I mention flashlights, widely offered on television not long ago, which did not require replaceable batteries. You shake the light and turn it on and it works. The light is not brilliant, but I've had two of these for years and they still work. That's important. The lens serves as a magnifier for the light. Whenever I know I'm going to be out at night – or even suspect that I might – I have a small **SureFire tactical light** in one of my pockets.

I also follow this practice when I'm going to be in any large building, a good portion of which, at least, is fully enclosed – like a convention center. If the power goes, there will be emergency lights, but these may or may not provide adequate illumination for personal safety. The **SureFire E1B Backup** is an ideal size and has a run time of 37 hours in the five lumen low-light mode, while the 80 lumen high beam run time is one and three tenths hours. Four inches long, with a pocket clip for ease of carry, it's a terrific light for my purposes. Versatil-

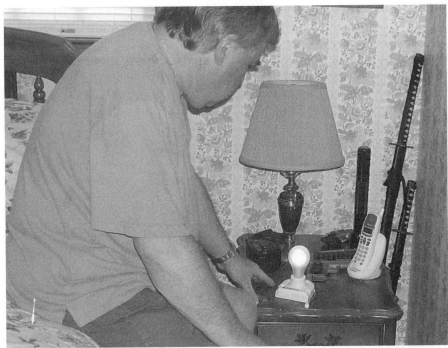

When the power is out, one of these handy, battery-operated Westinghouse stick-up lights can be dismounted and set on a table to provide the rough equivalent of a 40 watt bulb.

The Westinghouse battery-powered light bulb, turned on.

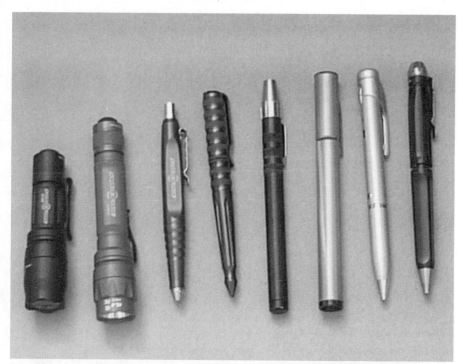

From left – the SureFire backup, Surefire L4 digital Lumamax and SureFire pen which can be used defensively, a Benchmade pen which can also be used for other purposes, a defensive tool which incorporates a spike that can be used for defensive purposes, a pocket telescope/microscope, a pen incorporating a two track tape for recording memos and another SureFire pen which incorporates a handy automobile glass breaker as the cap. All these versatile items are easily carried in a pocket or purse.

ity is always welcome in gear that can help you to stay alive and well.

Surviving Severe Thunderstorms

For some reason, people often tend to ignore one of the most potentially lethal weather phenomena we face: lightning. Lightning is electrical discharge associated with storms involving rain, but this type of static discharge can take place over intensely hot wild fires and is sometimes associated with dust storms or even the dust from a volcanic eruption. It travels so rapidly between a cloud and the ground that, as soon as it strikes, the lightning is traveling back from the ground to the cloud. The temperature of a bolt of lightning is more than 50,000° Fahrenheit, hot enough to turn sand into glass and well over five times the heat at the surface of the Sun.

People are struck by lightning every year. There are some few people who have been struck more than once by lightning and are still alive to talk about it. If you are caught outside in a thunderstorm, however, don't count on being one of

A thunderstorm being born. Photo courtesy NOAA.

The temperature of a bolt of lightning is more than 50,000° Fahrenheit. Photo courtesy NOAA.

them. Don't take shelter under a tree; don't be near golf clubs, rifle barrels or any metal objects. Get to the lowest piece of ground you can find, staying away from fences and the like. Lie flat and protect your head and face.

Although you can't outrun a tornado in your car, you can stay safe from lightning strikes in your car, which is grounded. If you can safely get to your car, do so. If you are near a permanent structure, better still. Lightning rods and surge arresters are available from several sources and the structure of modern homes may very well not include any provision for defense against lightning strikes. If your home does not incorporate protection from lightning, you should investigate taking appropriate measures to correct the situation.

There are over 100,000 thunderstorms per year in the United States alone. Yet the cause of a thunderstorm is not fully understood, only the mechanism of how it works. Some contend, for example, that solar activity has a direct bearing on the development of thunderstorms. Indirectly, of course, solar flares and the like aside, the Sun's effect on the creation of a thunderstorm is obvious.

Although lightning is rarely associated with snow storms, the thunderstorm itself is a warm-weather phenomenon, the Sun heating the Earth's surface and setting the stage for what amounts to a match between the rising surface air and the colder air aloft.

When liquid and ice particles collide within a cloud, they cause a buildup of static electricity. This creates a spark, and lightning is the manifestation of that spark. Thunder

A spectacular photo of cloud-to-ground lightning. Photo courtesy NOAA.

is not always present with lightning. Thunder is the result of the air surrounding the lightning bolt being superheated. The air expands suddenly, making the familiar booming sound.

Warm surface air heated by the Sun rises, of course, toward the colder air mass aloft. This convection gets the thunderstorm rolling, fueling it, the reason why most severe thunderstorms take place in late afternoon and early evening in the warmer months, when there's been plenty of chance for heat buildup.

The storm begins. As it gathers momentum, other storms form, this becoming the "line of thunderstorms" to which the TV weathermen and the National Weather Service refer. Most thunderstorms are not severe. Severe ones, however, which occur regularly enough, produce cloud to ground lightning and may produce winds in excess of 60 miles per hour. Such storms may also foster the creation of hail of various sizes.

Hail can do anything from looking interesting on a hot summer day to putting tiny dents into the hood or roof or trunk of your car to punching holes in the roof of your home. Larger hail sizes, depending on where you happen to be, can fracture your skull or even kill you. Consider the measurement system utilized by NOAA's Storm Prediction Center, in which hailstones are compared to commonly known objects:

HAIL SIZE (in.)	OBJECT ANALOG REPORTED
.50	Marble, moth ball
.75	Penny
.88	Nickel
1.00	Quarter
1.25	Half dollar
1.50	Walnut, ping pong ball
1.75	Golf ball
2.00	Hen egg
2.50	Tennis ball
2.75	Baseball
3.00	Tea cup
4.00	Grapefruit
4.50	Softball

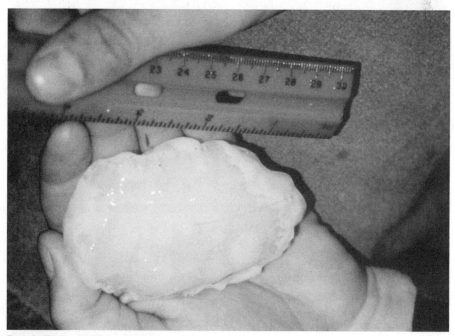

Baseball-sized hail is no joke. Photo courtesy NOAA.

Imagine a ball of ice the size of a softball striking you in the head or striking the windshield of your moving car. Softball-sized hail is, thankfully, not that common. Penny-sized hail is relatively common, however. Enough hail can fall to make it appear, for a short while, that there has been a sudden snowfall in the middle of a heat wave.

Thunderstorms carry with them heavy rains. These heavy rains, in turn, have the real potential to cause flash flooding in low lying areas from the sudden engorgement of creeks and streams.

Damaging straight line winds, hail, heavy rains and moderate flooding can cause lots of headaches, of course, but don't qualify as a disaster – although you certainly should seek shelter when a severe thunderstorm is about to strike. But lines of severe thunderstorms are the perfect incubation system for the development of tornados.

Surviving Tornados

The wind speeds of the greatest hurricanes pale in comparison to those in an F3 or greater tornado. An F5 can have winds twice as strong as the strongest hurricane.

Tornado intensity is measured on the Fujita Scale (or Fujita-Pearson Scale). An F0 has winds between 40 and 72 miles per hour. Winds in summer thunderstorms can easily gust in that range. Stick your hand out the window of your car as you are accelerating to highway speed and you can experience it. Damage is minimal. An F1 can flip over cars and uproot trees with its winds ranging from 73 to 112 miles per hour. F1 Tornados are 25 percent or more common than any other category.

An F2 packing winds from 113 to 157 miles per hour will tear off roofs, destroy outbuildings and turn over mobile homes. F3 tornados have winds clocking out between 158 and 206 miles per hour. They are rare. This is a good thing since they peel away exterior walls and roofs, collapse metal buildings and do the same to wooded areas and cultivated fields.

An F4 almost never occurs. With 207 to 260 mile per hour winds, almost any building will be destroyed and heavy objects will be flung through the air, becoming horribly dangerous and destructive missiles.

Although, God forbid, there may be a tornado someday that surpasses the F5, the damage it could cause would be incalculable. An F5 destroys everything in its path, ripping entire upper stories off those buildings it doesn't level. Wind speed runs between 261 and 318 miles per hour. F5s are the rarest of the rare.

When big earthquakes strike, there are invariably aftershocks, some nearly as intense as the earthquake itself. The problem with tornados is that they can come in pairs, even swarms. Imagine two F2s coming at you or a half-dozen tornados ranging from F1s through F3s assaulting your town, your home. Exposed without proper shelter, human survival would be all but impossible.

This tornado has almost touched down near Lakeview, Texas. Photo courtesy NOAA.

Traditionally, people in tornado-prone areas – some of these areas are called a "Tornado Alley" – have prepared with a storm cellar being a designated place of refuge, as well as a great place to store stuff. Storm cellars aren't always available, however. When there is a tornado warning, you should follow the steps you have hopefully practiced with your nuclear family.

You should have, at the very least, an **emergency water supply**, an emergency **First Aid kit** and emergency **lighting** ready to go. When there's a tornado watch announced, one member of the family should, at once, check that the flashlights work, the First Aid kit is properly stocked and the water supply is fresh. Preferably, you'll have a basement.

When the warning is announced – meaning that a tornado has been sighted and is quite possibly headed your way – go to the basement, positioning yourself away from windows that are not securely shuttered and away from things like hot water heaters, which could rupture, given the right circumstances. Try to pick a place in the basement beneath a solid structural support for the floors above. It's wise to have a heavy blanket or quilt to cover yourselves in the event of any flying debris.

If you haven't got a basement – and, a great many homes these days do not – find an interior room of the house on the lowest level possible, hopefully a room without any windows. A bathroom might be good. A sturdy closet will work. If you are able, position yourself beneath a door frame or similar structural feature in order to further protect yourself from falling debris. If you are in a bathroom and you would not be putting yourself at risk from shattering shower doors, actually climbing into the bathtub isn't a bad idea, unless there's a great deal of lightning and the tub is one of the old cast iron models.

If you are going to ride it out on a ground floor, pulling a mattress over yourself can be a very good idea. If you have no sturdy interior room that will work for you, get under a heavy table and pull that mattress over you.

If you live in a mobile home or otherwise have no truly suitable shelter, find the lowest spot possible outside – like a ditch – and lie flat, protecting your head and face. If you can, pull a heavy blanket or something similar over you.

If you are driving, *do not* attempt to outrun a tornado. They change direction and guessing wrong will get you killed. Pull over to the side of the roadway, if possible, and turn on your emergency flashers. Find a ditch by the side of the road and lie down flat, covering your face and head with your hands and arms. If you have a coat or blanket handy, cover yourself for added protection from flying debris. Stay as flat and close to the ground as possible. If you're a religious person, you'll probably be praying.

Once the tornado has passed, assess damages, if any, and see if you can help anyone who didn't fare quite so well. Remember that more tornados may be on the way and you may have to give a repeat performance. If you are outside and there is electrical activity, you should seek shelter immediately. As the Weather Service points out, if you can hear thunder, there is lightning close enough to strike you.

Basic Compass Use

The question lurks in the back of the mind of every non-compass user: "What good will the arrow always pointing north do me if I don't want to go north?"

Once you get past that question, using a compass for basic land navigation is really quite simple. Various compasses have various features, but the common thread is that needle pointing north, drawn to the north because of the Earth's magnetic field, no matter where on Earth you happen to be (unless it's a rare anomalous area generating a magnetic field of its own).

The Survivor Dry Box from MTM incorporates a compass on the lid and a reflective surface on the exterior of the underside. It comes in two sizes and you have color preference. This is an extremely handy item.

Now, since the needle always points north, merely face in the same direction as the needle and line up your symbol for "North" under the needle by turning the body of the compass. If you want to follow Horace Greeley's famous advice and "Go West, young man," all you'll have to do is turn your body 90 degrees to the left. Make certain to turn the compass in your hand so that the needle is still over your symbol for north. If you keep that needle and the symbol for north aligned to your right as you walk forward, you'll be heading west.

If you performed the exact same procedure and turned ninety degrees to your right, you would go east, merely by keeping the needle and your symbol for north properly aligned on your left. You can go south by turning a full one hundred eighty degrees. You'll note that the needle and your symbol for north are pointing directly at you.

What if you want to go somewhere that isn't straight north or south or east or west? Depending on the style of compass you have, there will be marks or actual degrees or both shown on the dial (if it is free-floating) or on the exterior edge of the case. Determine which mark or number of degrees is in line with the direction in which you intend to travel. With certain compasses, you can line up a front and rear sight and observe exactly which degree designation is aligned with your sights, your sights "aimed" at some prominent object in the right direction. Just always keep the needle over the symbol for north and try to keep the compass level each time you take a reading. Some compasses lock the motion of the needle to prevent damage; so, make certain that your needle is unlocked before trying to use the compass.

If you are using an automobile compass, be alert to the fact that such compasses are made to be read from behind rather than from above. Therefore, when you see the compass designation "N" pointing toward you, it does not mean that north is behind you, but rather in front of you.

Since you don't want to stare at your compass non-stop, you should pick a landmark of some sort, one quite obviously noticeable, and one that is aligned with the direction in which you travel. Walk toward the landmark, periodically checking that the needle and your symbol for north are properly aligned.

If you are using a map, no problem. Set your map on a flat and level surface and place your compass on top of the map. Look at the map to determine how the cardinal points are presented (which way is north on the map). Move your map until the compass needle pointing North is aligned with the map's North. For this sort of map use to work getting you from point A to point B, you have to have a pretty good idea of where you are starting out. So, before doing this, you may have to pick a land feature which is visible to you and is identifiable on the map. If possible, go to that feature and orient your compass to your map from there. You will now know where you are on the map and can use the map by using your compass as explained above.

If you can pick out two prominent physical features that are identifiable both in reality and on the map, you are in business and have saved yourself a hike. You sight your compass to obtain the number of degrees of angle from where you are standing to the first physical feature. Note the number and set your compass on the map, keeping the needle over north. Draw or scratch a line between the map representation of the physical feature you selected and the point on your compass dial or case with the same number of degrees as you "sighted," picking up the compass and continuing the line, perhaps to the edge of the map. Repeat the process for the second physical object, shooting the "azimuth" to the object and drawing the "back azimuth" to your compass. If you did this properly, where the two lines cross, you have completed a triangulation and pinpointed your location on the map.

Is this all you need to know to be an expert with a map and compass? Of course not; but these basic skills (in the absence of a magnetic force, large metal objects, powerul electronic signals and the like) will get you through most simple, practical land navigation. If you purchase from **Brunton** (www. brunton.com), one of the leading makers of high quality compasses, a handy booklet is included covering compass use beyond what is touched upon here. Go to a gun show or Army store and you will probably be able to obtain a copy of **Department of The Army Field Manual FM 21-26, Map Reading**.

There is more advanced direction finding equipment, which can pinpoint any location on Earth within a few feet. It's called **GPS**, standing for Global Positioning Satellite. GPS is standard or optional in automobiles and is used by the military for everything from land navigation to missile targeting. The GPS satellites broadcast a locator beam that your handheld or vehicularly mounted GPS device can receive. Your device will show you exactly where you are, just like a compass, only more precise.

In the event of a major disaster, however, it is possible that such technology, no matter how impressive, might be temporarily disrupted. GPS satellites would make natural targets for missile strikes, of course, helping an enemy to seriously interfere with Command and Control. Satellites could also be affected by a large solar flare. And a lot of the GPS tasked satellites are getting old and need maintenance, at the least. Keep that reliable compass handy, just in case!

Rumors

The Internet is a marvelous tool and a fantastic means of communication. It is also the greatest source ever for rumors concerning virtually everything and anything. There are rumors that there is something wrong with our Sun because of the prolonged period of minimal to non-existent sunspot activity. There is likely not a thing wrong with the Sun. There are rumors about political figures, Ends of Days prophecy, pending legislation that would attack Freedom of Speech or the Right to Keep And Bear Arms, movie stars and singers – it sometimes seems as if it would be hard to find something about which no one was spreading rumors.

During one of the civil dislocations of the late 1960s in Chicago, there were so many rumors swirling about that a Rumor Central service was started, where people could phone in and tell the person on the other end of the line what rumor they had heard. In turn, the Rumor Central call-taker would try, within the realm of what was practical or the calling center knew, relate what was really going on, dispelling the rumor.

Failing a Rumor Central that you can approach for valid information, there are quite a few things that you can do for yourself. If you know someone who has an involvement with the field the rumor addresses, contact that person directly. I was assured, for example, in a dire sounding email, that a piece of onerous legislation affecting part of the Bill of Rights was being sneaked through Congress. The legislation talked about in the email sounded terrible and the man who sent me the email was someone whom I respect. I immediately got on the telephone and called a friend whose job and passion it is to keep up on such matters. He assured me that the legislation had been unsuccessfully proposed some two years earlier and never went anywhere. Rumor shot down.

If you don't happen to have a well-qualified expert's phone number, but you wish to validate or dismiss a rumor, dismantle the rumor into its constituent parts. Research these separately, as needed, and then start "Googling" the question. If it is a popular rumor, in no time at all you'll locate websites partially or wholly devoted to it. Start reading, fact-checking and fact-matching. If the rumor has substance, you'll learn more and fill in some of the blanks. If the rumor is founded in nothing except innuendo or the failure to examine the facts or check sources, you'll discover that, too.

It's good to be informed, but rumors are another matter. Disinformation, whether unintentional or deliberate, can do a great deal of harm and often serves to lead to more trouble than there is already. Before you pass along a rumor, do some checking. If there's truth to it, you'll be passing along more accurate and useful information. If there's no truth to the rumor, you'll be doing everyone a service by stopping the rumor's travels right then and there, before anyone wastes any more time on it.

A Weapons Reference Library

Because of legal liability, firearms manufacturers generally trip over themselves offering you free replacement copies of their instruction manuals. Many of these operator's manuals can also be found online, this being especially true for older firearms.

Procedural issues can also be addressed. We recently undertook a project involving adding an important accessory to a shotgun I had not disassembled for years. I found a source on-line which showed the disassembly procedure in terrific detail, much more quickly and more graphically than a manual could have done. I reviewed it, checked a few steps and seriously smoothed out the procedure involving the new accessory.

Once it is determined which weapons will be involved in any possible defensive scenarios – whether at nuclear family, extended family or prepared community level – undertake to secure a full reference library pertinent to these weapons. The more portable, just in case, the better.

Something I have done for decades is accumulate **instruction manuals** associated with my personal firearms and house them together in a simple zippered case. I will soon be changing the case to something more water-resistant. Even with guns that I have used for years and years, I still keep a manual. In the normal course of events, if I need to identify a part for replacement or I've temporarily forgotten a procedure, I have a handy reference. In a post-disaster survival context, these manuals serve not only my needs but, should someone else in my nuclear family, extended family or prepared community require familiarization, these manuals will help.

Law enforcement agencies and military units generally share a great deal of commonality of weapons. Your families or communities are not para-military groups, just normal people trying to get themselves positioned to make it through to the other side of an unpleasantness. There is likely to be little commonality of weapons, so cross training with trusted individuals is something that should be periodically practiced. It can also be fun. A handy portable reference library is an information source that you shouldn't be without.

Care and Maintenance of Firearms

Sharon and I were making a video a few years ago and, with the help of some friends, in a full day's filming, we test fired more than 30 firearms. The majorities of these firearms were borrowed for the purpose of the video presentation and would be returned when the video was completed.

The more unfamiliar a firearm is to you, the more difficult it can be for you to field strip (partially disassemble) it for inspection and cleaning. Getting those guns cleaned so they would be ready to be returned was something that translated into a great deal of work.

Firearms that can be used in defense of your loved ones and your home need to be properly maintained – not babied, but cared for. Extractors (devices which catch and tug the spent cartridge case from the chamber so it can be ejected) have been known to break at the point where the actual hook is positioned at the extractor's leading edge. If the extractor does break, the firearm will usually cease to function reliably. Spares of these and other parts prone to breakage or loss should be secured for each defensive firearm that is to be used for possible post-disaster defense. Little things like grip screws can fall off a table or get lost in the dirt if you are outdoors. Rear sight blades can shoot loose. Springs can fly away. Without some of these parts, the gun will still function. Without others, the gun will have become an expensive and rather awkward club.

Similarly, guns need cleaning and lubrication, although certain guns do not require as much attention as some others. For decades, I have used **Break-Free CLP** with all my handguns. You must be careful to pick a lubricant that will function properly with your weapon in your environment and climatic conditions. For example, some lubricants will pick up and hold fine dust, of the type our courageous men and women of the U.S. Armed Forces encounter daily in the Middle East. Some firearms are more sensitive to the condition of the lubricant. The AR-15, the common designation for the civilian semi-automatic-only version of the military M-16 series, is lubricant sensitive. Cold weather can cause some lubricants to thicken and become gummy. This will also lead to weapon malfunction or failure.

If you live in an area of serious climate extremes – like northern Minnesota in the winter or the Florida Everglades in summer – you will need to find a lubricant that will protect the gun without interfering with function. Go to your local gunshop and/or range and inquire of people in your neck of the woods what their preferred lubricants are and why. Check out product information on the internet. Try a small container before you go after the giant economy size. And, there's nothing wrong, in most cases, in maintaining your firearms the old fashioned way – solvent and gun oil.

Cleaning rods for long guns will be commonly of the type that comes in segments which are screwed together. I've always liked the chain variety. Whenever possible, the cleaning patch should be started in the barrel so that it is pushed or drawn toward the firearm's muzzle. With a brass chain, just drop it down the barrel from the muzzle, position your cleaning patch and pull the chain and the patch forward. You don't have to have a separate rod or chain for each caliber; however, with larger bore sizes, you do have to make certain that the cleaning patch is making sufficient contact with the interior diameter of the barrel to actually clean it.

Assemble your cleaning gear in some sort of case you can pick up easily and take from one location to another or even take into the field. If you can still find cloth baby diapers, they are the best thing for wiping down the exterior of a firearm after it has been cleaned.

The Contents of the Boogie Bag or Bug-Out Bag or 72-Hour Kit

There are as many different suggestions for the contents of an item that has at least three names as there are disasters during which this item is intended to assist you. Our standard personal kit – which is very small and handy – contains many of the items commonly suggested for inclusion. Because of the size of our kit, and where it might be taken, there are other items which could prove vital which must be reserved for the larger boogie bag. To help readers to more fully understand the concept of the bag, Sharon pointed out that a pregnant woman will make up such a bag a few weeks before anticipated delivery. The contents will, admittedly, be a bit different.

Human beings need **water**. Most people will recommend a gallon of water a day for all one's needs in normal climate conditions. Since a gallon of water weighs just under eight and one-half pounds, the 72-hour concept cannot be adhered to concerning water – unless you're really strong. At the beginning of the 72-hour period, the water – exclusive of the container or containers in which is it housed – would weigh a hair over 25 pounds.

Take a single gallon at most over and above the individual-sized water bottle in your kit and secure and learn to successfully operate a small water filter. The **Katadyn Pocket Filter** is right there at the top of the line. You can take

A partially packed bug-out bag. This bag is an ideal choice and made by Blackhawk!

virtually the most disgusting water you might be able to envision and purify it to drinkability. Once you've reached your destination, the filter will still be handy to have around. Remember that the water supply is linked in with electricity to run the pumps and computers to co-ordinate their function. Knock

Ahern using the Katadyn Pocket Filter which can handle the filthiest water and make it safe and drinkable. No mud puddles being handy at the moment, Ahern is pumping water from a pan in the kitchen sink.

Canteen cover, canteen cup and one-quart GI canteen with a bottle of water, the modern canteen.

Ahern drinking some purified water, thanks to the Katadyn filter.

out the power grid or take down the Internet or both and the water will stop flowing sooner than you'd like. That means you'll be relying on what water you have and what water you can purify.

Depending on your physical strength and the terrain you might encounter, you'll have to determine the actual capacity of your **large water container**. The standard G.I. canteen carries one quart of water. Two-quart models are available. I'd go with multiple containers, so the weight can be balanced out in the bag and, in the event one container is rendered

Ahern uses the Katadyn Combi Filter. This filter can be attached to most faucets so you don't need to pump or you can pump from even turbid water. Service life for this filter is approximately 13,000 gallons, with 60 gallons per activated carbon element.

un-useable or its contents compromised, you'll still have one or more additional containers to rely on.

If you are so inclined as to have a firearm – I am – you'll want **extra ammunition and spare magazines or speed loaders** (devices shaped like a revolver's cylinder which are designed to load a cylinder full of cartridges into

Ahern with the Blackhawk! Bug-out bag that can be slung over the shoulder or carried with handles. The bag has lots of pockets and is sturdily made.

your revolver in one motion). Prepared individuals who habitually go armed will generally carry two spare loaded magazines for their firearm of choice. If I were carrying my Glock 22, for example, plus two spare magazines, I would have 15 or 16 rounds in the weapon itself and an additional 15 fifteen rounds in each of those magazines. That would most likely be more than adequate to get me to my destination. To be on the safe side, however, two more spare loaded magazines would afford me an additional 30 rounds and weigh precious little (the actual weight of a single magazine loaded with 180-grain hollow points is 11 ounces).

You'll want to include a **change of clothes**. Under some disaster conditions, clothing could become affected with dust or more serious contaminants, or you could be soaked to the skin from an emergency sprinkler system or just because it's pouring and there wasn't time to get the emergency hooded raincoat out of your kit. Morale is important under emergency conditions, too. A change of clothes can positively affect the way you feel. You'll also want a good, heavy **sweater** or a heavy **sweatshirt**, the zip-up hooded kind of sweatshirt affording you the broadest range of comfortable wear-ability. Obviously, in winter time, and especially in areas with severe temperature extremes, you'll want something more than a sweatshirt. Indeed, an **all-in-one** of the type often worn by hunters, mechanics and other persons who must be physically active under cold conditions (think **Carhartt** or something similar) might prove to be ideal. For added comfort, you should include a change of **underwear** in your change of clothes. In extreme cold temperatures, that underwear might be thermal.

You'll want **leather or heavy cloth gloves** for a variety of reasons that will become apparent as you use the gloves. Make sure to get something sturdy, yet something which will allow you to perform a wide range of tasks with the gloves on. In cold weather, try gloves with glove liners. The old GI mulehide gloves and woolen liners aren't the warmest things in the world, but they'll do.

The Special Forces Medical Handbook is another piece of essential equipment and a good thing to take with you in a bug-out bag. The boots are from Blackhawk!

Even if you don't like to wear a hat, have a **hat or bandanna** available for a head covering. In cold weather, a disproportionate amount of body heat is lost through the top of the head. A head covering may help also keep rain and sun off your face or face and neck and will help to keep insects and dirt out of your hair. If you are bald or shave your head, you'll need to be especially careful concerning possible sunstroke.

Footgear is vital. A pair of **comfortable cross-trainers or hiking boots** should be in your car and/or with your kit whenever possible. A few pairs of clean, dry athletic or cushion sole socks will be worth their weight in gold. Try **Thorlo's hiking socks** (www.thorlo.com).

You'll want a **fixed-blade sheath knife**. You won't need or want something huge. One of the modern tactical knives with one piece construction and sturdy handle scales made from G-10 or Micarta will work. The biggest I'd go in overall length is about 13 inches total with a blade a little under seven inches. The smallest is about seven and a half inches with a three and one-half inch blade. Avoid a double-edged knife here. For this application, single-edge construction is vastly more practical and safer for you to use afield.

A good quality stainless steel or tool steel blade is preferred. Make certain the knife has a reliable and sturdy sheath which will allow it to be worn as need be. Yet a fixed blade and sheath combination which is small enough to be slipped into a pocket can be handy, too. As with the folding knife in your kit, try not to skimp on quality. A knife is, first and foremost, your most basic survival tool.

The Blackhawk! Small Pry is a multifunction tool for getting into and out of places.

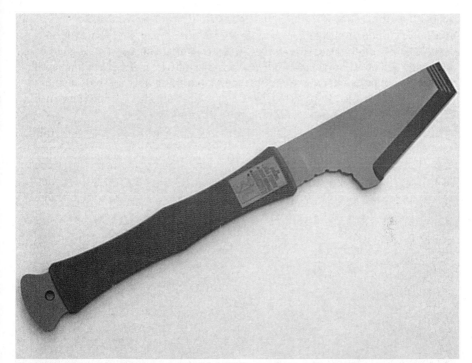

Flat shot of the Small Pry from Blackhawk! It can be used to hack your way through a doorway or window and is excellent rescue equipment.

Notice the edge on this Blackhawk! Small Pry.

You'll want a knife sharpener that is small, lightweight and easy to use, even if you are no great shakes at knife sharpening. I use the **Hunter Honer** from American Delta Products. It'll even sharpen many or most serrated edges and works great with a Benchmade combo edge, for example. It weighs next to nothing and is inexpensive.

Ahern sharpening a Benchmade knife on the Hunter Honer.

Energy bars are a part of your standard kit, but for the possibly protracted use of the bag, you'll want more than that. There is foil packaged tuna that requires no cooking to be pleasantly edible, for example (alas, not as good tasting as Sharon's tuna salad), and the little cans of **deviled ham** and the **cans of chicken** that don't require a can opener. The tops that you pull off these little cans are sharp. Be careful not to cut yourself. Similarly, you may find some application for these lids because of that sharpness. There are **cans of fruit** to be had, similarly packed; or you can go to the instant energy of **dehydrated fruit**. Just make certain to pack this latter in some sort of airtight container, so it doesn't spoil.

Tylenol and/or **aspirin**, in larger containers than in your kit, should be included. Even if you don't take aspirin for headaches, you might consult with your doctor to make certain he or she has no problem with you keeping aspirin handy in the event of a possible heart attack.

Better pack some **Murine** to soothe irritated eyes. Rubbing just makes your eyes feel worse and can do damage. After exposure to tear gas, for example, rubbing your eyes can break blood vessels. **Orajel** tooth desensitizer is a good thing to have along in the event of dental pain and, for more serious problems – a crown comes out or a filling is lost – you'll want the **Den Tek Toothache First Aid Kit**. You can find it at Walgreens.

You'll want a **toothbrush and toothpaste**. **Floss** is part of your kit. You'll want **wound pads and other medical supplies** in the event of traumatic injury. I like the **Personal Trauma and Advanced Trauma Kits** from Cavalry Arms. You'll find them in Dillon Blue Press Magazine (www.dillonprecision.com). The Personal Trauma Kit has 15 grams of Celox granules to combat serious bleeding, a pair of protective gloves, a Chem-Light light stick, a roll of Kerlix and six inches of emergency bandage.

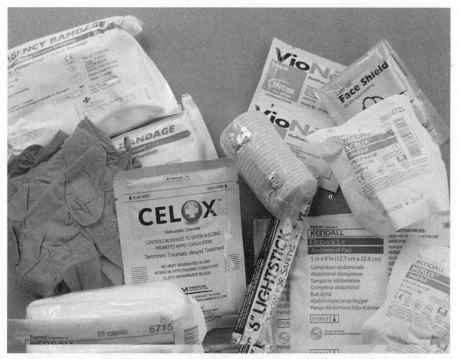

The Advanced Trauma Kit assembled by Cavalry Arms and sold by Dillon Precision contains the same sort of gear used in military trauma situations.

Don't forget **soap** and **hand sanitizer**! Likewise, **latex gloves** are always good to have along.

You'll want a **notebook** and **pencils**. You can sharpen pencils with a knife, but pens can run out of ink or prove defective. You may need to leave notes, jot down co-ordinates, etc.

You may wish to stash a pair **sunglasses** in your bag. As noted elsewhere, a **high-performance flashlight**, whether the high lumens tactical kind which can temporarily disrupt an assailant's night vision or the police style flashlight – but larger than the shirt pocket variety – is a must.

To round out the contents of the bag – remember, you want to be ready for anything – I recommend the **Glock entrenching tool**. The handle telescopes for ease of carrying, and it's hollow, holding a limb saw that's Teflon coated. Because the handle also folds, the angle between the blade and handle can be locked in whatever position you wish for handy digging or scraping. A small **axe** of the kind one can buy at a hardware store is a good plus. I prefer a **tomahawk**. Either will do double duty as a tool or a weapon, but the tomahawk is a little more versatile and usually lighter in weight.

The Photon Freedom Micro-Light is amazingly bright. This shot was taken in full daylight.

This American Tomahawk Company Viet Nam Tomahawk is a lightweight and versatile axe which can be used for a wide range of routine or defensive purposes and is in use by many personnel in the US Armed Forces.

Include a pair of **armored binoculars** – they needn't cost an arm and a leg – or a **telescope**, in both cases for enhanced distant viewing and scouting of terrain you must cross. A **First Aid book** and a good **survival manual** will give you something to refer to and, if you can't fall asleep, allow you to read and get your mind off your troubles. In that regard, the waterproof **New Testament Bible from Bardin & Marsee Publishing** weighs only a pound.

A **radio** which will allow you to get, at the least, the local NOAA weather radio broadcasts (which also should include Homeland Security/FEMA updates) is vital. These can be had with a crank for hand-charging the batteries. Certain models incorporate a powerful light for illumination and some include a siren for signaling. Some models will allow you to connect your cellular phone to the radio for re-charging its battery.

Whatever you call the bag, the contents can get you through to the other side of most crises and help save your life.

Non-Food Items To Consider

Before the Attica Prison Riot of September 9, 1971, it is reported that inmates were allotted one roll of toilet paper per month and one shower per week. I won't even comment on that, except to say that you are not going to want to get along on one roll of **toilet paper** per person per month in your nuclear family as a natural or manmade disaster plays out.

Toilet paper is just one of the things that should be stockpiled to provide an adequate supply in case of an emergency.

The person in charge of grocery buying and accurately determining how much food to put away for a specific period of time when such stores might be needed must also calculate what non-food items will be needed and how much of such items to put away. He or she must also determine what sort of rotation schedule should be followed with such supplies.

Let's take a few examples, and we'll start with the toilet paper. Always plan for the worst and hope for the best. It should be assumed that, under stress and eating different, perhaps more nutritious food, one's digestive system may change and, along with that, one's bowel habits. Those habits could go either way. You'll have to plan for a greater than usual need, rather than the opposite, when you are determining how many rolls of toilet paper per person for how long. Watch for sales, of course.

Things such as **toothpaste and dental floss, bar soap, shampoo and other products for maintaining good personal hygiene** must be calculated, to be sure, but there are also some subtle things. Lots of men and women are seriously into lip balms. Younger people particularly are subject to pimples and a bothersome pimple that is scratched with dirty hands can become infected. A lot of guys, myself included, shave every day, no matter what, assuming that water's available (I always shave in cold water, so not having hot water available for that wouldn't bother me at all) along with **shaving cream** and a **razor**.

We feel better when we can be ourselves. For that reason, assuming the space available, certain items some persons might deem frivolous need to be part of the emergency supplies inventory as well. A woman, for example, may feel less herself if she is without this or that **cosmetic or skin cream**. What does it hurt to inventory such items in a home emergency preparedness context? Not a thing. Mental health can prove far more fragile than physical health during episodes of severe stress. Little things can make people feel happier, divert attention from a possibly grim present to something much more pleasant, more normal, if only for a moment.

Make a list of all the items regularly used by your nuclear family. If you are part of an extended family or a prepared community, coordinate with those other persons who are working up similar supply lists. Check your list for anything that is impossible to inventory or just isn't worth the space. Remember that what you may consider ridiculously dumb or useless might be what someone else considers important. Be flexible.

If necessary, sit down with the various members of the nuclear family and have each of them old enough to do so make up a list of things they consider so important that they should be included in the emergency stores you're putting up. Don't get testy when your teenager wants to make certain there are enough **batteries** so he or she can play a **handheld video game** or listen to **CDs** through their ear buds. Remember the mental health aspects of what might lie in store. Having to be "turned on" all or most of the time works better for some of us, but not for all of us.

Whether it's reading a favorite **book** or having a couple of handfuls of **M&Ms**, if it makes someone in the nuclear family feel better and works no harm against anyone else in the nuclear family, include it, if possible.

You might suggest to your nuclear family that everyone keep a **diary or journal** – guys will probably consider the word "journal" more masculine sounding – in the event of a manmade or natural disaster. Such an event is life-changing, to be sure, and details dim with the years. Sometimes, too, just being able to talk about something – often not to someone, but just being able to put it into words – can have a marvelously salutary effect. To this end, pick up some **notebooks** – not ring binders – and **pens and pencils**. Make certain to acquire double-lock plastic bags of sufficient size that a notebook will easily fit inside for moisture and dirt protection. Stressing that no one should take a

chance in order to get a photo, you may wish to encourage your nuclear family and the extended family and prepared community to develop a photo log or record of events. And of course a **digital camera** can have many uses in an emergency, from recording places and conditions to documenting the apprearance of your family members in case they become lost.

Decks of cards, crossword puzzle books, crayons and coloring books for the little kids – all these are important. In most dangerous or unpleasant situations, it seems, there are periods of frantic activity punctuating lots and lots of boredom and waiting around. Whatever can be done to lighten spirits is a plus. Such diverting activities – responsibilities which have nothing to do with survival and impart order and normalcy to an unfamiliar and scary situation – will not only be good for everyone's moral, but will, after the crisis has passed, prove an emotionally valuable record.

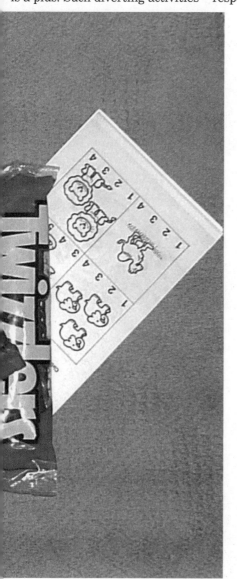

Candy, a child's favorite toy, a coloring book and crayons and a deck of cards for the adults are essential elements of a family's mental survival gear. Normalcy is important.

CHAPTER 21:
FINAL THOUGHTS

When I was a young man, there was a popular stereotype of the proper intellectual who would puff on his pipe, thrust a hand into the pocket of his tweed sportcoat with the suede elbow pads and begin his erudition by saying, "These are perilous times...." Well, these times *are*.

Radical Islamic fundamentalists want us dead or enslaved; there is no middle ground with these sociopaths and they will never stop. Our climate is doing something, but no one – awards and prizes notwithstanding – quite knows what, because the entire issue has been politicized beyond reason. We may have already entered into the next global pandemic. Our nation's debt level is insane when you consider that a trillion dollars is a thousand thousand (million) thousand (billion) thousand (trillion) dollars; we cut back on spending for things which could save the entire human race from oblivion – like observation tools for keeping track of Near Earth Objects – in order to spend money we don't have on programs we don't need.

The cancer of socialism is metastasizing throughout much of the body of Latin America. Dictators in various pitiless fiefdoms around the world are busily building missiles and working to be able to mount nuclear weapons aboard them while the rest of the world counter attacks these rogue regimes with carefully worded not-too-harsh language and possible sanctions, rather than stopping these tyrants cold.

As this is written, the record and near-record flood waters that swept away more than eight lives in Georgia and the southeast are receding and the rains have stopped. Federal Bureau of Investigation agents appear to have cracked two separate weapons of mass destruction bomb plots against buildings in the heartland of America. Still another possible terror plot, a far-reaching bombing conspiracy linked to Al Qaida, appears to have been interdicted. It has just been announced that Iran apparently has a secret nuclear facility, one which, at the very least, can help accelerate their likely program for the production of nuclear weapons.

These are perilous times, all right. Get ready to take care of yourself and your loved ones when the need arises. Make sure you read this book *before* you need it, so you can make it through to the other side of disaster.

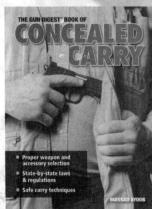